Outcome Management

Achieving Outcomes

for People with Disabilities

Art Dykstra Jr.

High Tide Press ✝ 2008

PUBLISHED BY HIGH TIDE PRESS
Homewood, Illinois

08 99 96 95   1 2 3 4

Outcome management: Achieving outcomes for people with
disabilities / Art Dykstra Jr. – 1st ed.

ISBN 978-1-892696-08-3

(previously published by High Tide Press, ISBN 1-57654-000-6 and
ISBN 0-9653744-0-8)

Book design by Alex Lubertozzi
Illustrations by Scott Bjelland

Printed in the United States of America

FIRST EDITION

To my best friend

and number one Boojum—

C O N T E N T S

Acknowledgments

TO ME IT IS DOUBTFUL THAT ANY MEANINGFUL contribution or accomplishment is the result of one person's work. Such is the case of this effort as well. It reflects the ideas and contributions of a great many individuals.

The members of Trinity Services' Board of Directors and Trinity Foundation—Robert Borgstrom, Paul Brumand, Barbara Hall, Dillard Harris, John Hauck, William Lipsey, William Long, S. Joseph Matesi, Raymond McShane, Al Olson, Herman Roche, Anne Schauland, Kenneth Stromsland, and George Troha—have given much of their time and talent to improving the lives of persons with disabilities. For their support I am most grateful. A special thanks to Joe Matesi and George Troha, who serve as the chairpersons of the two boards, respectively. Also, a special thanks to Ken Stromsland, who served as the primary recruiter in bringing me to Trinity.

To my colleagues and members of Trinity's executive group I owe a great deal—Steve Baker, Trudy Curtis, Tony DiVittorio, Debbie Gustafson, Lori Hausherr, Ann Ihrke, Holly Janczak, Sharon Parker, Arlene Purdy, Mike Sieling, and Amy Tabor.

Bob Sandidge, Anne Ward, Irine Hwang, and Dan Bertram provided much encouragement. Linda Hayes served as a valuable sounding board and clinical consultant. Also, thanks to Charlie Smith, who provided the necessary transportation.

People from my past have also contributed to this book in ways that they might not fully understand—Walter Fisher and Chuck Keysor, now both deceased, Roger Wyatt, Bob Agranoff, Roy Butler, Gene Glader, and Al Hunsicker. Not to acknowledge all of the staff, wherever they may be, of former Region II of the Illinois Department of Mental Health and

Developmental Disabilities would be an error of great significance. Also, Jim Nelson, Craig Kronholm, Duane Gibson, Tim Williams, Nate Cohen, and Don Blackburn.

A great deal of appreciation is owed to Jim Gardner and the staff and Board Members of the Accreditation Council for People with Disabilities, the rich and stimulating dialogues within this group are memorable experiences. Also, thanks to Doreen Croser and the Board of Directors of the American Association on Mental Retardation for allowing me to represent them to the Accreditation Council.

A special thanks to Donna Bolz, who was able to input these efforts on the computer and now reads my handwriting better than I do.

To Scott Bjelland, for his assistance and creativity in providing the artwork, I am in debt.

Finally, there is Alex Lubertozzi, who helped shepherd me through this project and provided valuable feedback and assistance. I am deeply grateful.

—*Art Dykstra*

Introduction

OUTCOME MANAGEMENT IS ABOUT RESPONSIBILITY. Art Dykstra's definition of responsibility covers the imperative to know as well as to act. Knowledge precedes action, for there can be no creative action without understanding. The strength of this book is that Dykstra, as president and chief executive officer of Trinity Services, knows and understands people with disabilities, their families, and the service delivery system. This knowledge enables him to share his insights and suggestions for enhancing the quality of services for people with disabilities and the employees of organizations providing those services.

Outcome Management is a first-hand, personal account of leadership taking action. Dykstra integrates his personal day-to-day experiences with an understanding of leadership and organizational behavior.

This book focuses on the synthesis of information to arrive at a greater comprehension of the phenomenon in question, whether it be the person receiving services, staff, middle management, or top leadership. With this focus on understanding and synthesis, Dykstra questions how services and supports for people relate to the outcomes they desire. Dykstra's confident grasp of the issues enables him to write, "It was embarrassing to realize that we were spending so much of our time and resources on disconnected activities that had little to do with what the person really wanted."

Everything counts, he says, and for people receiving services and supports, everything especially counts. Following the discovery of what people want through self-assessment interviews, Dykstra points out that, "An organization's staff...cannot stay the same, nor can the organization. It was the experience of talking with the people served which motivated us to go the next step and examine all the organization's practices."

The strength of this book is Dykstra's ability to connect his understanding of people served with his knowledge of what leadership and organizations can do. In making this connection, he provides the reader with a wealth of applied, innovative approaches that work.

The major contribution of *Outcome Management,* however, is the reframing of existing practice, policy, and procedure around a different rationale. Dykstra examines traditional practices such as the job description, organizational specialization, leadership, assessment, service planning, and records, and suggests a larger, more meaningful perspective for each. This book offers creative alternatives to managing the status quo.

Personal responsibility, a learning environment, and intelligent risk-taking produce innovative leadership and competent, compassionate management. Dykstra's ability to develop and sustain a culture of continual improvement in a large community-based service delivery system provides the basis for this narrative.

Outcome Management will challenge you with new possibilities for leading the organization, motivating employees, and facilitating outcomes for people with disabilities. Remember, these are not theoretical possibilities—Dykstra has used and sustained these programs and applications at Trinity Services for more than eight years. Take these principles and make them work for you.

—*James F. Gardner, Ph.D.*
Chief Executive Officer
The Accreditation Council

preface

Raising Zucchinis

"We can identify our values by hard thinking."

—*Ralph L. Keeney*
Value-Focused Thinking

ARDENING IS A FAVORITE hobby of mine. Turning the soil, seeding, even weeding are all enjoyable activities. To see the late summer or early fall outcomes of new potatoes, squash, and Brussels sprouts is indeed a quality experience.

This past spring, I decided it was time to engage in the pursuit of raised-bed gardening. I built several beds, being sure not to use "treated" lumber—after all, the experts of *The Mother Earth News* and *Organic Gardening* had advised against using such materials because the chemicals would leak into the soil and cause harm. I dug the ground underneath each of the raised beds and discovered excellent black soil. I fertilized the beds following all the recommended formulas.

What to plant? My wife really loves zucchini and so to surprise her I thought I'd try something new. She enjoys slicing zucchinis and putting tomato sauce and other tasty things on top and baking them in the oven like pizza.

Personally, I don't like zucchini, but when I found seeds for round ones I knew she would really be pleased. I had never seen this type of squash seed before and, although they were a bit expensive, I made the purchase.

Abiding by the seed packet instructions, I gently kneaded the soil and planted each seed very carefully. I remember my thoughts while I planted: "This is going to be an unbelievable harvest—why, you can get ten thousand zucchinis just by emptying the seed packets on the ground. What will I do with all the zucchinis? Who else can I give them to?"

As the growing season unfolded the most gorgeous blossoms you could imagine covered the ground. The beds formed a giant rectangle of golden trumpets.

Then the vines appeared, vibrant green, a fabulous turgor. They were not average vines; they were great vines.

Harvest time came and, despite having the right seeds, the right soil preparation, no weeds, great blossoms, and great vines, I had no zucchinis. I was a failure. I felt worse than any gardener could.

Even as I share the thoughts that follow, I do not know what went wrong. Perhaps it was a lack of pollination; maybe the seeds were infertile. I still don't know.

What did occur to me, however, was that the experience could very well be a metaphor for many organizations today.

The services and supports we provide, or the business we conduct, may take place in state-of-the-art buildings, architectural masterpieces with numerous floor-to-ceiling windows and carpeted stairwells. Staff may be well trained and, in some instances, even well paid. Certificates appear; mission statements grow; satellite offices emerge. Everything is going according to the strategic plan, but frequently no one knows if anything meaningful has occurred. Has the organization borne fruit? How does anyone know? Is there an expectation of harvest? If so, is it in proportion to the time, energy, and resources invested?

This book is about achieving outcomes in organizations that serve persons with disabilities. It reflects the thoughts and efforts of many people who are committed to doing a better job of what they do—every day. As a result, it is a book borne out of experience, not out of theoretical discourse.

chapter one

Why Outcomes?

"This year we plan to run and shoot. Next season we hope to run and score."

—Billy Tubbs, former Oklahoma Basketball Coach

BAND WAGONISM IS SORT of the American way—grab the latest gimmick, swallow the magic pill, recite the five-step formula, latch on to the current management fad, send three staff members for the price of two to the one-day seminar now coming to your community for only $99.95.

Hope for the quick fix and, when it doesn't happen, blame the employees for being dumb, uninterested, or disloyal. In the best of circumstances staff, returning from these learn-it-all-in-one-day seminars, remember three new jokes for a few days, or, in some instances, may learn some of the tricks of the trade, but they never learn the trade.

Sadly, it is often the top executives who take their staff and organizations to such wayward destinations. And then, of course, cynicism sets in and employees discuss the new flavor of the month, the new slogan, the new vision and quietly share the same thought: "This too shall pass."

Once, during a graduate class that I taught on executive leadership, one of my students said that her company had tried MBO (Management by Objectives), Theory "Z," Quality

Circles, Pursuits of Excellence—why they had even tried the Golden Rule—and that didn't work, either.

This kind of thinking probably leads to the rumored message in a suicide note left by a frustrated manager, "I can't stand it anymore—and I don't know what *it* is."

It is my fear that the present interest in outcomes is for many people the same old search for a magical answer, the teaspoon that holds the healing antidote. What is tantalizing about outcomes, as a construct, is that they sound easier than all the standards and paperwork associated with a process orientation. Perhaps you don't have to worry about documentation, data, or degrees any longer. You simply win, come out ahead of your competitors if you hit the target. And targets are readily available—high status in the community, accreditation, certification, program halls of fame.

Charles Handy suggests in *The Age of Paradox* that we live in a time when most important issues are paradoxical. Managing paradox depends upon your ability to see relationships between many variables and to understand the interactions as a system.[1] This is what Peter Senge, in *The Fifth Discipline*, terms "systems thinking." In most complex systems, acting upon one variable does not simply change that variable, but sets off a series of reactions, mostly unseen, which may lead to results that contradict your original intention.[2]

So it is with outcomes; an organization cannot consistently achieve outcomes, whether in the management sphere or with the individuals served, without being concerned about the systems and processes that lead to the outcomes.

A colleague and communications consultant in the field of disabilities, Anne Ward, observes that, with respect to conceptualizing and emphasizing outcomes in providing supports and services to individuals with disabilities, "They are a lot simpler. But that does not mean that they are easier."

The ideas and strategies for organizational improvement found in this book are indeed simpler, but by no means easier.

A discussion and consideration of outcomes raises all kinds of questions—more questions, in fact, than answers. Some of the issues raised are very philosophical means and ends considerations. For example, supported employment may be one person's outcome or end—the responsibility and status that come with a job—but another person's means—having the financial resources to rent his or her own apartment.

Outcomes are about the bottom line. What is really being measured or accomplished from a business perspective—return on investment? James Cribbin, writing in his book, *Leadership*, suggests other returns: "Return on ideas, return on improvement and information, return on individuals, return on interactions, return on interface, return on integrity, return on 'inthusiality'— which is one part enthusiasm and one part vitality."[3]

The outcomes of any organization invariably reflect the values and principles that are practiced in its everyday functioning. The outcomes achieved might represent the power needs of the chief executive officer or, in other instances, reflect the lack of leadership. In today's economy, it follows that the sought-for organizational outcomes are shaped much more by a desire to satisfy the customer.

Harvard University Professor and psychologist Ellen Langer offers many helpful insights in a consideration of outcomes in her 1989 book *Mindfulness*. She believes that one of the things wrong in society today is the emphasis on outcomes. She shares many examples from the educational world.

Talk to kids today and they are not excited about the process of learning. Parents everywhere, especially those who are achievement-oriented, bribe their sons and daughters to get A's and B's. Very few parents bribe their children to get C's and D's—and so getting A's and B's seems to be the outcome of our

6

educational system. The importance of developing a questioning mind, the ability to generalize from the textbook to the real world, the joy of the journey, the process of learning and not just reaching the destination remains, for the most part, underdeveloped and unappreciated.[4] The same thing is happening in organizations; managers bribe employees to complete their assignments, to come to work on time, to achieve "quality," without ever conveying or explaining why.

This emphasis on just achieving outcomes leads to mindlessness—mindlessness that is evidenced in, as Langer says, "not being open to new possibilities, treating information in a single-minded way, thinking that our perceptions are the accurate ones, having rigid categories of understanding."[5]

It's difficult to exhibit a mindful attitude when all you're doing is paying attention to outcomes—while ignoring the processes that lead to them or the circumstances that surround them.

What happens when our only concern is with outcomes that disregard the connecting variables? The following experience sheds light on the inherent flaw in being solely outcome-oriented.

I have enjoyed fishing for more than forty years. During that time I have acquired numerous lures, rods, reels, and tackle boxes. My transport is a fourteen-foot aluminum boat with a ten-horsepower motor.

It all began with this boat and motor. To catch more fish I quickly realized I needed to purchase a trolling motor, that way I could move quietly and sneak up on the fish I was trying to catch. Because subscribing to numerous fishing magazines would help me succeed in catching more fish, I got them all. I always read the articles with titles like "Five Proven Ways to Catch More Fish this Spring (this Summer, this Fall, this Winter)" first.

It wasn't long before I needed a fish finder that lights up and beeps when your boat is over an intended conquest. Soon after

I had to trade this one in for a newer model, complete with a microchip that allows me to gain a written record of the spot and circumstances of the find.

I was now closer to my objective of catching a fish with every cast.

A year ago my wife, seeking to pay me back for all the fine zucchini I tried to grow for her, gave me an incredible Christmas present: flying fish lures. Perhaps you've seen them advertised on ff. They go under docks and trees, fly through the water away from you and locate the spot where the lunkers are hiding in ambush. Little boys fishing from shore held me in awe.

Recently, my son Thane called from Rhode Island to tell me of his discovery that would be of even greater help in catching more fish: Fish Scents. They're guaranteed to attract more fish or your money back. My favorites are "Crayfish," "Crawlers," and "Lunker Leach."

Just recently, I purchased some new spider web line for a more sensitive touch. Even the weakest bite will be detected.

Sorry to say, a troubling thought recently entered my "catch and release" world. It is possible that in the not-too-distant future I will purchase the long awaited fish call, or the coolest fishing jacket (the one with all the pockets), or the computerized bait and tackle rig, or the sonar snare—and I'll catch a fish every time I cast.

What fun will that be? The same could be said of golf. What fun would it be to record an eighteen every time out? With such technologies one could save a lot of time—but what would remain?

If there were no hurdles in our lives, nothing that defined our humanness, nothing to learn about in journeys to be made, we would become a mindless people in a mindless world.

Why have outcomes recently become so popular in the field of disabilities? I suspect that several forces have converged to create the interest. It is not simply another example of trying to keep up with the Joneses of the business world.

Many staff and administrations have become dissatisfied with a rigid conformance to process standards as the criterion for achieving quality. Efforts to comply led to enormous amounts of paperwork and the demise of common sense. In an effort to demonstrate an understanding of the residential care standard that, "menus should reflect a variety of foods," program staff are reprimanded for serving turkey to program participants the day after Thanksgiving. Perhaps the only people in the United States who do not eat turkey the day after Thanksgiving are vegetarians and those people living in intermediate care facilities for the developmentally disabled.

Standards sprout from other standards, not from an organic need to improve quality.

Such adherence to standards is an outgrowth of process evaluation that leads to the frequent complaint of employees that they spend all their time on paperwork.

Another factor contributing to a desire to try another way is the realization that all of this focus on how things are done and documented hasn't resulted in any significant return on the resources invested. Individuals with disabilities are not necessarily living more abundant lives and achieving their personal goals, even when all the process standards are met. In some instances, compliance with the prescriptive rules and regulations actually interferes with the attainment of more desired lifestyles.

Even when the elaborate processes of quality control and statistical quality control yield column after column of numbers, many now realize that numbers are not results.

Today, most organizations are trying to write or, with the aid of a computer, print out their way to quality programming. The Original Plan comes first, and if for some reason that fails, what comes next is the Plan of Correction. Some organizations even use a Plan of Action to monitor the Plan of Correction.

The quest for quality ritual is widely known: every employee who might have any concern or relevance signs everything, along with his or her job title and date. Elaborate policy and procedure manuals are not considered complete until they include signed statements from each employee acknowledging that he or she has read the above and will carry out the duties as required.

Next come the check sheets—the length and breadth of which are usually determined by the extent of management insecurity or paranoia.

Then come the quality inspectors. Their job is to check up on everybody—are all forms properly filled out? Filed in the appropriate places? Completed on time?

Almost everyone involved—managers, professionals, even the program participants themselves—have had enough process for at least one important reason: the process has not improved quality. More trees have been needlessly killed, more Xerox machines burned out, and more expensive file folders purchased, but nothing very meaningful has happened.

Outcome Management is a new way of thinking; it emphasizes the whole as well as the parts. As Peter Senge observed in *The Fifth Discipline*, it is the management of dynamics over detail.[6] And yet, Outcome Management is based on a full understanding of the need to be concerned about process. You cannot have an outcome without a process.

In the field of disabilities the important individual outcomes for the persons served or supported are based on careful processes of individualized decision-making.

An outcome is a result, a consequence, or a conclusion. It is not a shortcut.

The next eight chapters provide insights into the primary organizational elements that are the basis for Outcome

Management. Quality, organizational culture and relationships, risk-taking and exploration, learning, and personal responsibility are all essential components of an outcome-producing organization. The remainder of this section focuses on systems concerns—relationships among employees, managers, and customers, as well as the effects of other organizational variables on these relationships.

The essential element for an outcome approach to management is a culture that desires and actively pursues continuous improvement.

chapter two

Continuous Quality Improvement

"We are what we repeatedly do. Excellence then is not an art, but a habit."
—Aristotle

S OMEONE ONCE SAID THAT power accrues to men and women who have the most evenings to spend. A similar observation could be made concerning quality— quality accrues to those organizations whose leaders have the most evenings to spend. But this observation is not about being or becoming a workaholic or master of perfectionism.

What it captures is parallel to the Biblical injunctive to pray without ceasing. A commitment to continuous improvement embodies a pervading and prevailing attitude and belief that things can always be done better. With such an outlook, it is impossible not to think about how supports, services, or circumstances could be improved. This inclination is always with you even though it may not always be in your conscious awareness.

It troubles me to realize that many managers and clinical practitioners in the field of disabilities believe that continuous quality improvement is a new or recently-invented concept.

Since the beginning of civilization, there have been those who have worried about their accomplishments and the functioning of the organizations to which they belong. Perhaps up until recently their concerns have gone unnoticed or unheard.

A friend of mine suggested that the internal imperative to do better is really a curse—the curse of knowing right from wrong. Those managers called to thought as well as to action must therefore act to correct or improve the wrong when they see it. As Burton Blatt, one of the most outstanding reformers in the field of disabilities, stated many years ago, "To observe sorrow untouched is to cause it to continue."

I believe that if corporate boards would have had the benefit of the presence of an artist or poet they would have taken the business of continuous quality improvement a lot more seriously a lot sooner. For it is the artist and poet who know best the struggles of complex dilemmas, illusions, and the shortcomings of the scientific method.

Quality as an ongoing concern is a matter of internal direction and unrest. It is continual and only pauses on occasion. Yet the world is full of deadlines and necessary ending points, and so paintings and sculptures are completed, as are treatment plans and the services provided.

For the person committed to ongoing quality improvement, the next day, the next reading, or the next appointment reveals that some element could be improved upon and a course of action is laid out to make such improvements. All such changes, however, do not occur that quickly, and improvement sometimes happens as a result of extended individual or organizational learning and growth.

In my experience, even in the most change-resistant organizations, there is an exception to the, "We've finally gotten it right, let's not change it" attitude.

The most bureaucratic or the most quality-conscious organization is never satisfied with the development of its forms. Forms are either being changed, about to be changed, or being recommended for change. In some situations staff members are so confused as to which is the better or most recent form that the forms in use become color-coded. "Don't pay any attention to the white ones," staff is told, "the green ones are the ones we're using now." Of course it's only a matter of time before the staff has to replace the green in its thinking with blue or yellow.

It is conceivable that in the "need hierarchy" of certain administrators, the need to make and revise forms comes right after the need for safety and security.

A commitment to continuous quality improvement is not only a commitment of attitude; it also requires energy and activism.

Somewhere in my earlier career I came across an idea that, with my slight revision, has stayed with me for years: "Great men and great women become great doing the things they don't want to do, when they don't want to do them."

Sometimes the conditions preceding improvement are painful and the practices needed to achieve the desired outcome difficult. The tasks and time may not be to our liking but action is still required.

Leadership is critical in creating and maintaining a quality-producing environment. Many authors have written and continue to write about the importance of leadership in quality improvement efforts. I will only focus on two important realities of management life; namely, that people *leak* and people *stray*.

Leaking

It is not enough to simply admonish employees to do it right the first time. In fact, telling someone to do something very rarely, if ever, works—especially with something as critical as an ongoing concern for quality. Teaching is a much-preferred course of action with plenty of time for questions and practice.

For some mysterious reason people simply leak. That is, the full understanding of a concept or intent seems to dissipate over time. As a result, there needs to be a continual spoken and written emphasis on improvement. The vocabulary needs to be part of everyday functioning and organizational behavior.

The example of Cardio-Pulmonary Resuscitation training illustrates this point. Who would feel comfortable, if the need should occur, to perform CPR five years after the training? Who feels competent five months afterwards? To be a capable practitioner one must engage in regular practice and refresher courses.

Such ongoing training has to enter one's life and become a life skill priority.

Because people leak they need to be refilled at regular intervals. In ideal circumstances, employees know of this phenomenon and seek to stay full on their own initiative.

Informing employees of the "whys" behind organizational policy and requested courses of action curbs the leaking process and establishes mutual respect.

Straying

Just as it is part of the human condition to leak, so it is natural to stray from intended objectives and purposes. Again, it is the organizational leaders who must constantly return the organization to its intended mission.

The most unusual example of straying that I have observed occurred at an institution serving individuals with developmental disabilities. Walking through the campus, I passed many buildings. Almost everywhere I went, staff members were standing behind facility residents who were standing, spread-eagle, against the sides of the buildings. Arms spread and upright, legs far apart, the individuals were taking enforced "time-outs" as punishment for their behavior. The staff stopped short of actually frisking and handcuffing them—probably because they could not remember the list of residents' rights (to be free from humiliation and restraint obviously weren't among them). It was one of the most perverse sights I've ever witnessed.

Employees stray and so do organizations. Goals are not hard to displace and before too long the organization is majoring in the wrong subjects. A committed leadership regularly brings the organization back when it strays.

A scene from the movie, *The Little Buddha*, provides an important insight into the task of maintaining the intended results in an organization. Siddhartha leaves his father's kingdom and renounces material possessions and pursuits of the flesh. After six years of living with a group of ascetics in complete physical denial, he overhears a musician floating down the river instruct his student: "If you tighten the string too much, it will break; if you leave it too slack, you can't play it at all."[1] This observation reveals the wisdom of the middle way to Siddhartha—a balance between the physical and the spiritual. The ideal tension is neither too taut, nor too loose.

It is the same in organizational environments; there must be just the right amount of tension on the structure and processes to deliver the highest quality services and supports.

The leader must know how and when to loosen or tighten the organizational strings in order for the sought-after outcomes to be accomplished. And just as the lute will vary in the direction the strings need to be adjusted, so will the organization vary. Organizational leaders must listen to the corporate instrument every day. A responsibility of great magnitude.

chapter three

Successful Relationships

"It all started when he hit me back."

—*Overheard*
(older brother defending his actions in church)

I T IS MY CONTENTION that the nature of our organizational relationships determines the extent to which an organization can achieve or implement Outcome Management. The primary problem with most struggling and frustrated organizations today is that they are not concerned enough about this issue to be genuinely interested in confronting it.

Every CEO can tell you that building and maintaining relationships among employees is a priority. Some even spend money on it. Actually, most strategies are of the "spend or send" variety.

One popular strategy is to bring in a consultant. Those who have not-for-profit rates are generally preferred. Once the consultant has been hired and a date set, middle managers are ordered to turn out their employees who "need to change the way they've been thinking about things."

The room fills, the consultant shares some new jokes or stories, group exercises ensue, and gladness ratings are completed and calculated. Everybody goes home, but nothing significant is different as a result. The "send strategy" is very similar to the "spend alternative." Sometimes it unfolds in the following way: the CEO calls his or her human resource chief or staff development coordinator and says, "Hey, are there any human relations seminars coming to this area? There are? That's great… Wow, you can't beat all of that for ninety-nine bucks, and it includes a notebook and certificate too? Great, we can put that in their personnel file—Public Health will like that. Let's send eight or nine people, and while you're at it give them a call and see if we can get it any cheaper… What do you mean, what am I looking for? I am looking for these %&#!@ [*choose your own adjective*] employees to change their lousy attitudes. They don't know how lucky they are. I should fire them all and get some good employees in here!"

These one-day-stands rarely include top management. After all, they don't need relationship workshops. Someone has to get the job done.

These managers believe learning is the equivalent of telling or giving directions. Because the work of the organization is so important, all learning must occur within the limited budget or be done by three o'clock so people can get home on time.

The very worried CEO may, on occasion, gather all the troops together to admonish them with threats and shows of strength.

I attended one such meeting and the CEO snarled, "If I'm going down, you're going down with me!" He, of course, did not realize that the employees already felt that they were all the way down and had nowhere to go but up. But the thought of the CEO going down raised many interesting possibilities and fantasies in the minds of the audience.

The question might be asked, "Why be so tough on the chief executive officers?" The answer is found in the increased realization on my part that top management can be very destructive and that to genuinely re-engineer, reorganize, or reinvent an organization, top management must be willing to participate in and support the changing of relationships. These executives must ask the questions: *How am I contributing to this problem? What must I change about myself so that this organization can change?*

In an Outcome Management-seeking organization, people are valued in spite of—and because of—all their individual differences, all of their ups and downs, and all of their wants and needs.

Top Management Relationships

The future of successful organizations will emanate from full partnerships among all relevant participants. Such partnerships are based on trust. Trust, in this context, consists of several elements: a concern for the whole, a willingness to share information, the freedom to speak up, credibility, and the recognition of competence.

A concern for the whole is vital to the establishment of trust. Each corporate member is aware that the organization comes first, before any individual program or department. To know that the other person will subordinate his or her needs for the greater good is a powerful motivation to do the same. On a practical level, it means that the program with only a few vacancies in the staffing plan refers potential employees to the program that has the most. It means allowing a staff member to take a promotional opportunity in another department.

A willingness to share information is another characteristic of organizational trust. Is information openly shared or vigorously guarded? Such information might be of a wide variation— the acknowledgment of problems, the status of the company's books, providing the reasons for the decisions being made.

Trust is also present when employees feel that they can speak up and disagree without fear of punishment. Some organizations actually have specially-designated times when staff can address, "What's wrong in the company? Or the department? What's holding us back?" Cribbin refers to these times as "barnacle-removing sessions."[1]

Trust also comes through credibility. Is there congruence between words and actions? Does honesty characterize organizational practices? People are willing to trust those who tell the truth. It is an organizational maxim that to tell the truth and have employees angry is better than to tell a lie, and have them hate you when they find out.

Organizationally, there is one other important element of trust that is signified by the knowledge that one's co-workers, boss, and subordinates are competent to carry out their duties. Knowing that people can perform at the level required not only breeds confidence, but also creates an environment in which risk-taking can occur.

As the CEO of a medium-sized organization, I am often away from the corporation. Representing the concerns and purposes of the organization externally can be very time- and energy-consuming.

Trinity Services is managed through a leadership group that has authority for the major programs and services offered. The group includes line and central support staff.

Every organization struggles with the natural tendency of managers to view their position or department in the organization as being the entire organization. To keep the organization as a whole in front of many corporate leaders is an ongoing challenge. In a similar manner, it is not infrequent that CEOs make the mistake of believing that the organization consists only of those top management staff who report directly to them.

To deal with this reality, as well as to confront such issues as competitiveness, diversity, and changing priorities, leadership staff at Trinity have developed an Executive Committee Partnership Agreement.

What these individuals have signed is an agreement as to how they will do business together. The group meets weekly with me in attendance, but also two other times a month without me. I do not ask for reports or for minutes from their partnership meetings. In this forum partners resolve differences and create common agendas, make recommendations, and seek to maintain the purpose of the organization as a whole.

As I have shared this experience with other colleagues it has not been uncommon to hear, "You can't do that. They'll end up talking about you and before you know it you'll be out of a job." Another frequent bit of advice from these same people is, "If you ever learn that one of your staff is talking to a board member you need to jump him right away. The next thing you know he'll be the CEO."

While I realize that paranoia may be an occupational hazard of a leadership position, it is not my view of the world that these individuals will conspire to steal my chair or organize some kind of fifth-column uprising. The organizational reality is that if individuals at this level of the organization cannot be trusted or trust each other, how can one expect employees at the operational level of the organization to trust one another? This group is a corporate model for other organizational teams; individuals must be free to meet and discuss important issues without suspicion.

Manager-to-Manager Relationships

From an organizational dynamic or effectiveness perspective it may be more important to be concerned about the relationships of managers across organizational units than the nature of the relationships within a given unit. For example, the sharing of resources is always a potential hot spot for conflict and discussion. The ways in which managers relate to other managers is of critical significance if the organization is to thrive.

In organizations that provide both residential and day services or supports, it is not uncommon for major hostilities to erupt between these departments. In some organizations the staff do not even talk courteously with one another. Scapegoating is a favored course of action and it permeates the entire staff.

"They didn't even do this." "They did that." "They won't do this." Vocational staff complain that a residential worker did not pack a sufficient lunch for one of the program participants. Residential staff blame the vocational staff for not telling them that an individual would be late getting home because of a picnic. It's no wonder that certain CEOs frequently rely on a deputy or associate director to mediate such conflicts.

Many managers assume the false notion that what they don't hear won't hurt them. It is important that managers spend time with each other, sharing insights, supporting one another, and developing collaborative efforts.

Chief executive officers are called upon, first of all, to keep peace in the valley. There are numerous instances—in spite of the belief that organizations serving people with disabilities are "doing God's work"—of incredible infighting and political battles. It is difficult to be outcome-oriented when staff members are preoccupied with turf wars or the next wave of reorganization.

Manager-to-Employee Relationships

If you ask employees what it's like to work for any organization, they are likely to answer based on the relationship they have with their boss. That is a fact of life. "This place sucks—no one ever knows what's going on. All they do is take advantage of you; they never help you out when you're hurting. No one tells you anything."

Of course the likelihood of positive feelings and experiences is also possible. "It's a great place to work. I'm trying to get my sister a job here."

In this regard it is not uncommon for first-line managers to become managers without any essential training or chance to practice. Frequently, they are tossed onto the playing field and before too long, when difficulties arise, resort to giving orders on the one hand or doing the work themselves on the other. Management training, therefore, becomes a high priority in organizations pursuing a course of Outcome Management.

I found the cartoon on the following page on the bulletin board of a large corporation. Perhaps even more interesting was the management memo posted next to it, demanding that "unprofessional" artwork and cartoons be removed from all bulletin boards immediately.

More and more management books suggest that, in the future, the prototypical organizational culture will emphasize a status of "constituent" or "member" rather than of "employee." This is no doubt a desirable evolution and a circumstance that will result in improved outcomes and morale.

Such an undertaking will be difficult, however, and take time as well as the commitment of all staff, if it is to be achieved. Most organizations will not be able to make the transition. It will be seen as too hard, too time-consuming. If pursued at all, before the halfway mark of completion, it will be given over to the newest way of doing it (whatever that turns out to be).

The artifacts will remain awhile, however. The associates dining room will have a new sign reading, "Members Dining Room," member key chains will still be floating around, "Member of the Month" pictures will be visible for awhile. The member softball team may even win a few games. Finally, however, the employees, especially the grumblers, will be sent off to new seminars and workshops.

You

Are

Here

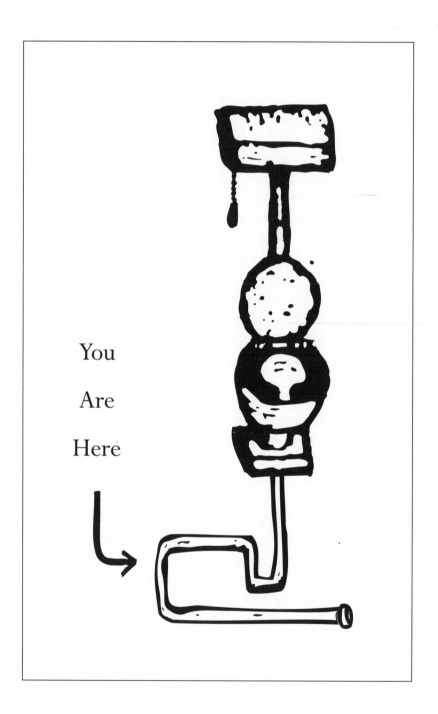

As Saul Alinsky, the master of community organizing, once remarked, "It's the same old shit, only the flies are different."

Employee-to-Employee Relationships

The employees who actually carry out the work of the organization—the treatment, habilitation, and education—are often referred to as the "hourly employee" (a term which probably captures the extent of their organizational value, or perhaps the extent of their commitment, or in some organizations, the measure of their turnover rates). These individuals still remain the key persons who fulfill the mission and purpose of the organization.

Who an organization hires is the most important thing that it does. Recruiting people with compassion, energy, and a sense of personal purpose clearly contributes to an outcome-producing work environment. Likewise, hiring people with positive attitudes certainly makes more sense than trying to teach courses in positive thinking.

Essential to fostering a positive and optimistic culture is to focus on the nature of employee-to-employee relationships.

Assuming that the organization strives to secure appropriate employees and uses the best techniques for employee selection—including behavioral interviewing—new employees should enter the organization with a clear understanding of the attitude, skills and performance levels that are expected.

In the family therapy literature, the observation is made that one should treat his or her spouse as one would want his or her children to treat others. This idea certainly applies to managers as well. Managers should treat each other as they want employees to treat each other. Role modeling can never be underestimated as a vehicle for learning.

The obvious goal is for employees to be responsible for their own behavior, and to treat each other as they want to be treated.

Employees who believe that they are doing meaningful work, who are using their creative and cognitive skills, and who know that they are being treated fairly, will do just that.

Employee-to-Client/Customer Relationships

It is rare for an employee who feels that he or she is being treated unfairly to maintain the personal strength and ability to provide high quality services. Thoughts and feelings of anger, frustration, or revenge disrupt a person's functioning. Similar things can be said about doing meaningless work, being over-controlled, or being grossly underpaid.

Often, direct contact employees will question the necessity of "running" a particular program after the skill has been learned, or of collecting data several times a day, when one time is sufficient. The staff needs to know that there is a "why" behind the services they provide. If management concludes that a questioning workforce is an uncooperative or lazy one, then it is thwarting the whole process of facilitating outcomes.

In order for individuals with disabilities to get better, grow, become more independent, and to feel secure, they must be served by a workforce that is supportive and psychologically healthy enough to do what needs to be done.

In general it is the staff that provides the instruction, guidance, and feedback that enables program participants to grow and gain skills so that they can live more abundant lives.

How employees are treated is probably the most essential variable in how the organization's customers are treated.

chapter four

Exploration

"A long-range weather forecast should be obtained before leaving, as weather conditions are extremely unpredictable."

—Unknown

 NOTHER ELEMENT CHARACTERISTIC OF an organization pursuing Outcome Management is the permission and freedom to explore and experiment.

In order for staff members to feel as if they can explore and try out new ideas they must be free from two major organizational impediments: the presence of an over-controlling authority structure and a mistake-punishing administration.

Over-Control

Many organizations are over-controlled. Again, it is not unusual to trace this phenomenon to the personality of the chief executive. The CEO's *modus operandi* may reveal itself in such practices as employee parking, rules concerning the copy machine, the number of duplicate documents made or requested, and whether employees receive their mail opened or not. Most employees can accept some of these indignities, but as higher order controls also present themselves, the enthusiasm to be creative begins to wane.

Higher order controls surround such issues as whether one has keys—and more important, to what? Purchasing freedoms, hiring authority, the type of information one may access, what permissions must be secured before taking action are other areas frequently over-controlled by management. Of immediate concern here is the freedom to initiate or suggest alternative program services or strategies, as well as management practices. Are employees encouraged to make proposals? Are their proposals read and responded to?

If there is an attitude of "this can't be improved upon," the whole business of exploration will be shut down. Other inhibitors are: "Mary says we have to do it that way;" "The regulations mandate it;" "The board said so."

Organizational practices often take on a life of their own, in some instances, long past the intended purpose. It is not unusual for staff members to continue sending copies of correspondence to employees who left the organization months ago. In terms of practices, it is not uncommon for regulations to change and find staff members not only following the new directions but continuing the old ones as well. Years ago, the State of Illinois mandated annual height measuring of all persons with disabilities served by the state. The rule was directed at children, but, for some reason, did not exclude adults, whose height rarely changed. State officials finally amended the regulation, but two years later I still observed staff members not only measuring adults, but converting the measurements from feet and inches to meters and centimeters.

Over-controlled employees are easy to spot—their heads are bowed and their spirits are broken. Such individuals will rarely engage in risk-taking activities and, when first confronted with a novel situation, will look through the index of the organization's Policy and Procedure Manual before doing anything. If, however, no one is looking, they will more likely telephone their fellow employees and ask them what to do. Personal judgment is very rarely called upon.

Punishment & Other Inhibitors to Creativity

The extent to which the organization punishes mistakes is the other primary inhibitor of creativity and experimentation. Once again, this is true throughout the organization, whether it be at the corporate or operating level. An individual publicly embarrassed or humiliated will not be free inside of his or her head to let the ideas fly—negative thoughts will dominate and lost opportunities will signal the failure of the day.

Mistakes need not be overlooked, but an attitude of, "What have we learned from this situation?" is the preferred alternative. The fact is we frequently learn more from our mistakes than our successes. In an organizational culture where mistakes are punished, they are also covered up, and so no one wins. The employee's self-esteem and integrity also suffer.

There are other organizational obstacles to creativity. An organization under siege from regulating bodies spends most of its energy in corrective planning, trying to outwit the inspectors. Likewise, an organization downsizing or laying off its employees rarely gives rise to new ideas. Energy that might otherwise be available for creative thought is consumed by bouts of fear or negative fantasies. The survivors, struggling with issues of guilt and separation, are rendered incapable of generating new or better ideas.

Fostering Exploration & Creativity

Exploration comes naturally to organizations seeking to continually improve. Better ways of doing things are always being pursued. Once again, this dynamic needs to be evident at all levels of the organization. Top management sets the tone of the creative environment. Ideas must not only be welcome, they must be sought. Conversations with employees should include, "What's your thinking on that?" "Now that you've been doing that for awhile, do you have any ideas on how this could be done better?" This is especially important with new employees. It should be a formality that, after sixty or ninety days of employment, the new employee meets with his or her supervisor and is asked, "What do you think about the way we are handling the laundry responsibilities? Or the household chores?" And so on.

All employees should feel that one element of their organizational responsibility is the responsibility to propose new ideas. The best ideas come forward from the employees who are doing the job that can be done better. Ideas should be expected from everyone.

In addition to the natural flow of ideas, however, in-house seminars and creativity workshops stimulate original thinking. Many techniques are available to foster such desired behavior.

Exploration can also be facilitated through the use of carefully selected consultants. A trained third party can assist staff to consider paths of organizational exploration that would otherwise not be taken. Experts in such areas as compensation planning, organizational development, or specific program areas can foster ideas and areas of opportunity.

At the management level, opportunity seeking should be stressed just as much as, if not more than, problem solving. Not all staff members are as capable of identifying opportunities as others, but employees can learn to be more creative through practice, support, and encouragement.

Exploration should concern itself not only with the operations of the present but with the possibilities of the future. The anticipation of and concern for the future rest primarily with the most senior management staff. In fact, Elliot Jaques, writing in *Requisite Organization*, suggests that employees should be paid on the basis of their responsibilities for the future. Because top management staff members are responsible for the greatest timelines, they would be paid the most.[1] It would be interesting to survey corporate executives and determine their time frames of concern. The time spans, one hopes, extend past tomorrow and the end of the fiscal year.

chapter five

Personal Responsibility

*"Ask 'em if they're looking for someone who's self-motivated, Ethel,
I don't wanna be making a trip down there for nothing."*

—*Willy*

I VISITED A SUPPORTIVE LIVING arrangement one early winter day and talked with the staff member who had the responsibility for managing the home environment. The persons living there all had substantial disabilities.

Noticing that the storm windows had not yet been pulled down to cover the screens, I asked her about the situation. "Yeah," she said, "someone needs to do something about that."

A few weeks later, I participated in a statewide meeting of organizational executives. One of the speakers was lamenting the lack of cost-of-living increases from one of the state funding agencies. The first audience response came from another executive director: "Someone needs to do something about that."

Not recognizing the need to take personal responsibility for our lives is apparently a mindset that still thrives. What of course happens in these situations is that we end up living our lives on the basis of the choices that others make for us.

Personal responsibility requires making choices and accepting the consequences of those choices. Personal responsibility is fundamentally about managing one's choices. As such, all of life's major issues pivot upon the choices that we make.

In his book *Choices*, Shad Helmstetter suggests that most of life's important choices fall into one of two categories, choices of *attitude* and choices of *action*.

Essentially, choices of attitude manifest themselves in the way you view the world, how you experience life. These choices come together in what is known as your personal perspective. He suggests that answering a series of four questions allows a person to gain conscious control of his or her attitude:

1. **How do I feel about this?**

   Asking yourself this question is the first step in gaining conscious control of your attitude—how you feel. Then give yourself a simple answer—if there is one—and consider it for a moment. How do you feel? Good? Bad? Okay? Happy? Unhappy? Excited? Angry? Nothing at all? Surprised? Relieved?

2. **How would I like to feel about this?**

   Next, ask yourself the second question. More positive? Indifferent? Understanding? Optimistic? Give yourself a clear picture of the feeling you would like to create, if you could.

3. **How do I *choose* to feel about this?**

   How you would *like* to feel about something and how you *choose* to feel about it are two different things. One is a "want"—the other is a choice.

   Try this for yourself and watch what happens. Ask yourself those first three questions. And when you reach the question, "How do I choose to feel about this?" give yourself *a specific direction of choice* that says, "I choose to feel '_____' about this," and fill in the blank.

4. **How do I feel about this now?**

   Finally, ask yourself the fourth question: "How do I feel about this *now*?" Chances are, with even a little practice, you'll find that you can, *at almost any time*, change how you feel about almost *anything* by making the choice to change how you feel.[1]

Helmstetter also suggests that there are four similar questions that, when encountered maturely, allow us to take greater control of our lives and daily action:

1. **What am I doing about this?**

   This question asks you to *ask yourself* what to do about the situation—the moment it occurs. It could be asked when you are meeting someone for the first time, when you are writing a business report, or when you are talking to one of your children.

   Because it is possible to do most of what we do in any given day without giving the matter too much thought, this question *really* asks us the question: "What am I programmed to do in this situation?" What would I usually do? How would I typically act? What action would I usually take, if I did not *think* about my next action *and choose it for myself?*

2. **What would I *like* to do about this?**

   If you could wave your wand, what would you really like to do? If you had your way and could do anything you wanted to do at this moment, what would it be?

   And this question also asks: "What should I do right now if I want to take the most effective, correct, worthwhile action that I can take?"

   All too often, we feel that we are subject to the whims of the world around us. We feel that we "have to" act in a certain way, or that we are "supposed to" do something, or that we are "expected to" do what others want us to do.

   Doing any of these—following the expectation—might be completely different from the action we would take if, at the moment, we thought about it and chose for ourselves what we would really like to do.

3. **What do I *choose* to do about this?**

   This question tells you: "What I do next is up to me." Making the choice for yourself puts taking personal responsibility back on you. It accepts your natural birthright to make choices for yourself.

When you ask yourself this question, you put yourself on the line. What you're actually saying is: "This is up to me. *I'm* making the choice. I choose to take personal responsibility for myself, and that's what I'm doing."

4. **What am I going to do about this now?**

Once you have made the decision to make a choice and act on it, you should find yourself taking action on your choice. That won't always be the case, of course; old programs die hard. There will be times when you will tell yourself that you choose to do one thing, and then find that your old programming convinces you to do another.

It can take time to get used to the fact that a strongly-stated personal choice is a powerful new program in itself. Old habits don't let go easily, and old programs love to step back in and regain control.[2]

In an Outcome Management-focused organization, staff members take responsibility for their own performance. They create or help to create the standards of measurement. They keep their own scorecards and are paid accordingly.

In *Servant Leadership*, Robert Greenleaf describes an incredible example of personal responsibility. It is the story of John Woolman, an American Quaker and writer who lived from 1720 TO 1772. As a young man he made it his mission in life to eradicate slavery from his own Society of Friends (Quakers). He did not denounce the slaveholders or rant on about the evils of slavery. "Gentle but clear and persistent persuasion" was his technique.

"The approach was not to censure the slaveholders in a way that drew their animosity," Greenleaf writes, "Rather the burden of his approach was to raise questions: What does the owning of slaves do to you as a moral person? What kind of an institution are you binding over to your children? Man by man, inch by inch, by persistently returning and revisiting and pressing his gentle arguments over a period of thirty years, the scourge of slavery was eliminated from this Society, the first religious group in America formally to denounce and forbid slavery among its members." By 1770, Woolman had accomplished his goal almost single-handedly. As Greenleaf asks, what would have been accomplished had there been fifty John Woolmans? Or even five?[3]

Each of us is confronted with situations that compel us to make decisions regarding our personal responsibility. Some are rather easy: *Should I return the money I received from the clerk's error? Should I pay the out-of-state parking ticket? Should I claim these contribution amounts on my income tax?* Other situations, however, are more complicated and far-reaching: *Should my spouse and I have children? Should I tell the truth regarding the accident? Should I have the operation? Should I publicly disagree?*

There is a conscious and introspective deliberation process that precedes action in thoughtful people. But once the choice is made, the person actively follows through. Not to make personal decisions is to begin to die from the inside out. The internal standards, values, and principles go first; the related outward behaviors soon follow.

Organizations are much the same. They die first from the inside and then from the outside. Integrity and purpose succumb to expediency while high standards are replaced by convenient and cosmetic ones.

True personal responsibility acknowledges the wisdom of the imperative, "Everything counts." I was first struck with the impact of those words in one of David Steinberg's comedy routines in which he made light of our tendency to be over-vigilant regarding trivial matters. Steinberg's character would walk around the house, straighten a picture on the wall, alphabetize the magazine rack, and say, "*Everything* counts." And indeed, there are those administrators—sometimes known as obsessive/compulsives—who drive their staffs to the brink of mutiny by obsessing over the truly unimportant.

But everything does count in an Outcome Management environment, and not just the outcomes—the first mistake made by folks who don't really understand the complex nature of process and outcome.

Everything especially counts when you are dealing with unusually vulnerable people—the little things as well as the big things. It is important how staff members greet the program participants each morning, how they hang their coats up, where they hang their coats up, and whether the people served participate in meaningful activities or not. Nothing is taken for granted.

Where the coffeepots are located is important. Who may drink the coffee is probably more important. How many times the phone rings before it is answered is important. Is the environment clean, cheerful? Have the flowers been weeded, the snow shoveled on time?

How are checks distributed and by whom? How much money does the janitor make? Where does the staff eat lunch? How expensive are the soft drinks in the vending machines?

How do the staff members in community-integrated living arrangements (CILAs) refer to the homes? At Trinity, we operate and serve more than thirty-five such homes and apartments. With this number of sites, staff, management, and I have fallen into the habit of referring to the homes by such names as Courtland House, Route Three, or Cedar House.

For some, this may raise the question: "So what?" But, when you realize that the way you talk affects the people you serve, you don't have to ask. What does a person being served in a CILA home say when asked, "Where do you live?" Does she tell them her address as we would? Or does she call her home by its work-site name that the staff uses? Probably the latter—and that is our fault. These properties may be worksites to us, but they are homes to the people who live there. That's an important distinction to make.

Everything counts, absolutely everything. This philosophy does not mean that one controls or micro-manages each of these events or activities, but rather that staff realizes the importance of every encounter with the people they serve. It is critical that little issues be dealt with before they become the problems, conflicts, or sources of bigger concerns.

If staff members learn to look for the variances in little things and it becomes part of their quality orientation, they will not stray into larger variances of uncorrected practices or attitudes. When you come back from vacation the same standards will be in place. Coloring, bead stringing, and ping-pong ball sorting will not have come back from the dead and re-invaded the program areas while you were away.

Bob Sandidge, a friend and colleague who is the president of Creative Core, is fond of making the statement, "You must be present to win." That he has succeeded in the field of multimedia presentations, publishing, and communications consulting and training attest to his ability to be present. To take responsibility for yourself you certainly must be in the present.

Being or living in the present doesn't mean rampant hedonism or the failure to plan for tomorrow, however. What it does mean is to be consciously attendant to the moment you are living, right now. To enjoy life is to extract all of its goodness as it happens.

Some of the people reading this book may not be entirely here right now. You may be worrying about what time you're going to go to bed, what you're going to do or wear tomorrow, or maybe you're distracted by events that happened earlier today. At any rate, it's likely that some readers won't freely experience being here on these pages, while others will.

We must learn to value the moment and concern ourselves less with managing it. I had a greater appreciation of this outlook when my father died. He was eighty-one and lived his life with an attitude of thankfulness and generosity. While my father lay in the hospital, his heart rapidly failing, I held his hand and we cried. Death was imminent and we both knew it.

"Art," he said, "it went so fast."

The next day he died. Life *does* go that fast. Not to enjoy the present is to forfeit much of life's potential. And so it bothers me when people talk about Wednesday as "hump" day or radio announcers proclaim it's "TGIF" day. To live Monday through Friday as something to be endured until the weekend is to discard seventy-one percent of life.

I want to distribute posters like the one that ends this chapter: "Thank God It's Today." If only more people could understand that personal responsibility is founded in treasuring the present.

Thank

God

It's

Today

chapter.
six

A Learning Orientation

*"Some people will never learn anything—because they understand
everything too soon."*

—*Norman Cousins*

I T IS EASY TO DISTINGUISH an organization that is committed to learning from one that is not. In a learningful organization, staff members read, listen to, and share books, articles, and audio-visual resources. They plan for and attend seminars and workshops. They take courses at local colleges, present papers at professional conferences, engage in research, and visit other similar organizations. New ways of doing things are continuously explored, and employees can't wait to share their latest ideas with colleagues or supervisors.

Simply stated, in organizations that are not concerned with learning, the activities listed above do not happen except episodically. In fact, in many organizations, learning is thought of as synonymous with training, and the training that occurs is compliance training. If the regulatory bodies require forty hours of training, staff members rarely get forty-one. "We can't afford it," say the managers.

And so, employees are scheduled in and out of the classroom environment, told not to chew gum in class and admonished to pay attention because there will be a test later. Photocopies of the daily attendance sheet will be placed in their personnel files.

That's so they have a record for the inspectors, they say, but the employees all know such documentation will be used against them if they ever make a mistake and someone wants to get rid of them. Staff development feels a lot like punishment and the staff would prefer not to go. After all, they say, "we already know that stuff."

The content, when taught, rigidly follows the established structure of the state regulatory requirements, whether it makes sense or not. And sometimes, the entire forty hours is taught by one or two people.

This, in all too many organizations, is what passes for learning, accompanied of course by the occasional excursion into the $99.95-a-day seminars discussed previously.

Any "free" training offered by state bureaucrats is likely to be well attended. This happens through staff roundups, whereby managers coerce unsuspecting staff members into going to the state seminars. The staff, of course, go for political reasons, not to learn, "They're probably going to take attendance and it's important for us as an organization to be seen in the audience." So the top administrators sit back in their offices, telling themselves that the employees are going for their own benefit.

Of course, what happens is that as soon as the attendance sheet is circulated and the organization name printed in large letters, the staff members leave the scene mentally. After lunch their bodies follow and they leave completely, though they rarely return to work (that's why such employees are so willing to drive their own cars to off-campus training events). The state bureaucrats are disappointed in the size of the post-lunch crowd—mainly because they have fewer course evaluations to turn in to their bosses to account for their day's work.

An important observation should be made at this point. Typically, many of the staff members employed as direct contact employees are available in the workplace because they did not do well in high school or did not enjoy it. It is certainly not because they are less intelligent or less motivated than those with college educations.

Placing such people in front of a blackboard in rows of desks, obligating written homework assignments, and calling upon individuals to give specific right or wrong answers may not be the way to encourage learning with these staff members. In fact, approaching learning in this manner—whether it be skill or knowledge acquisition—only leads to frustration for all parties. Other approaches and techniques need to be utilized. There are a wide variety of techniques for learning in a more creative and interactive way, including group or team projects, visits to other organizations, and interactive games. Peter Kline's book, *The Everyday Genius*, provides a rich source of new ideas for classroom alternatives.[1]

Clinical training is another area of potential learning that is frequently perverted into an excursion to compliance activities. Such training is frequently specified in terms of hours and regulatory content. In some states the completion of such requirements even results in an honorific status. After forty to 120 hours of classroom training, an ordinary person is transformed into a certified one. The rewards are often immediate for these employees—sometimes ranging as high as twenty cents an hour, if, of course, all the necessary paperwork has been completed and filed.

Does anyone care that the intended outcomes are not achieved in these organizations? Probably not.

A Learning Organization

The notion of creating or being concerned about a learning organization has accelerated with the wide acceptance of Peter Senge's *The Fifth Discipline*. Senge states that "a learning organization is an organization that is continually expanding its capacity to create its future."[2]

One of the foundation stones for managing an outcome-seeking organization is the presence of a learningful attitude. By "learningful" I mean imbued with the desire to learn and the joy of discovery. Curiosity is valued throughout the organization, and by expanding its capacity, the organization is more responsible for and able to control its own future. The substance of "capacity" is well developed by Senge and will not be discussed here except to note that this orientation involves more people-related issues than technical ones.

Critical to our capacity to affect change is an understanding that the future is also available in the present. What we are doing right now directly relates to tomorrow. In many important ways the shape of the future exists in the choices and decisions of today. As the French author Paul Valéry once said, "Not even the future is what it used to be."

Because this book concerns itself with the possibilities and applications of an outcome orientation to the management of supports and services to individuals with disabilities, a corollary thought to Senge's observation is offered: a learning organization is an organization that is continually expanding its capacity so that the people served or supported can create their own futures.

To me, this is a powerful propellant towards wanting to become a learningful organization. Without a learningful attitude, staff cannot hope to assist individuals in a meaningful way. Many of the people served in organizations today do not have the ability to create their own futures without the assistance of others. To help people with disabilities create their own futures—what an exhilarating challenge. If such an organizational purpose could become translated into everyday practice, think of the significant differences that could be made in the lives of people with disabilities.

I am concerned that organizations that over-control their employees also over-control the people they purport to serve and support. Many even have preposterous client rules—*No talking on the assembly lines.* And then, there are the constant, insidious reminders: *Show me good sitting. Show me good waiting. That coffee is for staff only. That is the staff bathroom (you, the client, get to use the dirty one). It's not your turn yet. Showers are at seven o'clock. Stuffed animals are not normalizing. 'R'-rated movies are not allowed here. You can't talk to staff that way. If you do that again, I'll call your mother.* In all probability, this list could go on for several pages. Staff members in learningful organizations are mindful of these "rules" and constantly work to defeat them.

Individuals creating their own futures are likewise creating their own present. It's impossible to disconnect the two concepts, but many organizations try to do just that every day.

To step backwards to a previous discussion, if an attitude of "everything counts" prevails, staff members pay attention to the language they use and the practices they engage in. They are self-correcting, encouraging each other to do better every day.

A Vision for the Future

To entertain thoughts of a more desirable future is to have a vision. Unfortunately, this concept has also become a buzzword. I am concerned that the consulting groups who are conducting "vision seminars" in organizations today were, last week and last year, conducting burnout seminars, excellence seminars, quality circle seminars, and empowerment seminars.

Today, there are vision seminars for everyone—PTAs, church groups, country club members, and even consultants. It is ironic that I have not come across any mailers or advertisements that are directed towards the individuals with disabilities themselves, whereby they could be assisted in "visioning" their futures.

I don't deny the importance of having a vision. The concept has been around for a very long time: "Where there is no vision, the people perish." —*Proverbs 29:18*

Visions embrace the hopes that we have for an organization. They are not the same as goals and objectives, yet they are frequently equated in organizational language and practice.

Having a vision is to have some sense of transcendence in our lives and in our organizations. Visions create a powerful sense of meaning and enrollment. They emphasize the values and principles of our corporate as well as our personal lives. With such a governing frame of reference, an openness for new possibilities comes naturally. The processes undertaken originate from that vision and the merits of the hopes presented.

Mental Models

Having an organizational openness to new ideas, based on a vision in which all employees can enroll, leads to a willingness to examine our mental models of the world. It allows organizations to achieve far beyond what one person has characterized as the seven last words of a failing organization: "We have always done it that way."

Let me share a true story to illustrate the impact of mental models on our lives:

A friend of mine, Tim, was in town last winter. We were meeting somebody for lunch in downtown Chicago. It was the middle of winter and it was about twenty-five or thirty degrees outside. We were down by Lake Michigan where the wind often blows so strongly. After parking in the garage, we had to walk about three blocks to the restaurant. We got out of the car and my overcoat was in the back seat. Tim had his overcoat on and he said, "Art, your coat is in the back seat."

I said, "Yes, I know."

I locked the car and we took a few steps and he said, "Your overcoat is in the back seat."

"I am just going to leave it in there Tim."

"Look," he said, "the wind is blowing, it's cold, and you need to put your coat on."

"Tim you're making me angry. I'm not cold, but you're making me cold. I haven't even thought about being cold—we're just going two or three blocks."

As Stephen Covey has suggested, we carry our weather with us. Now, this may not apply when it is forty-six degrees below zero. But, to some extent, how cold you think you are relates to how you view the world. It has to do with where your focus of attention is and what you're thinking about.

If you don't believe me, try this: if you take showers in the morning, when you get out of the shower, sing the national anthem. If you normally just stand there and shiver while you towel off, don't do that. Get out of the shower, grab your towel and start singing. Concentrate on the words. Do you know what's going to happen? You're not going to be cold because you're not thinking about being cold. You are probably more concerned that your family members now think you've gone off the deep end. But, you have also changed your mindset.

Perhaps you have employees who, when they see the first flake of snow, get anxious and say things like, "I saw one, do you think they'll let us go home early?" The next thing you know, the employees are all lined up at the windows. They turn the radios on. "What's the forecast say? Better get out of here because I saw a snowflake." These people are living their lives in this negative fashion. I would like these people to work for someone else. That's my goal in life—to have them line up at the windows of somebody else's organization.

An organization interested in outcomes needs to worry about its mental models. Learning to think differently about the world needs to be at the individual, team, and program level, in the minds of every staff member.

The Importance of Poets & Scientists

In order for organizational values to be alive in the employees, there must be a convergence of those ideas and beliefs that can be characterized as philosophies of life and those concepts characterized as philosophies of science. This is certainly true in the field of developmental disabilities. In fact, the two forces are the basis for most of the work that is attempted or accomplished—normalization theory and behavior analysis.

The stage may be better set in these organizations for a recognition of the importance that feelings, emotions, and subjective experiences contribute to an organization when combined with the facts and the desire for scientific objectivity.

Learningful organizations balance the fervor of determined data seekers with questions of meaning. Organizational poets are often concerned with notions of how the present affects the future and how the parts affect the whole. They temper the tendency to emphasize the parts that characterize the work of many would-be scientists. And so in organizations that embrace learningfulness, the relevance of folding towels to a person's life is questioned. How do all of the programs fit together? What sense does it make to be at step nine of a fourteen-step bed-making program for five years? Even if the data is honestly recorded for those five years, what's the point? In organizations that seek the answers to these questions, the significant life goals of the individual are pursued.

Employees, while concerned about humanness, purpose, and personal preferences, however, do not reject the contributions of science in outcome-oriented organizations.

48

I would predict that learningfulness would increase in those organizations that regularly conduct applied research. Being involved in research investigations reminds the staff that it does not possess all of the answers. The persons served or supported do not have to be called into isolated instances of hypothesis testing if there is a general culture of curiosity and learningfulness.

Celebrations

Learningful organizations have regular celebrations not only for the staff but for the people they serve. It is a tragedy of organizational programs that often the individuals who spend a major part of the day in training programs, following habilitation plans, being on step five of a fourteen-step program, do not know when they have learned something. There are no celebrations of accomplishments, just the next program, the next class, the next objective.

Many times the isolated learning objectives never unite in a meaningful whole. There are grooming programs, tooth-brushing programs, dressing programs, and change-making programs, but the programs always run separately and not always in the order of use or importance. Bringing the programs together so that the person served knows that he or she can more capably go out on a date, for example, very rarely happens. Staff members wonder why counting all the trials and missed attempts is so important. To not chart is to be punished, and perhaps even terminated. It is not unusual, therefore, for the charting to become more important than the successful achievement of outcomes.

The blues are a favorite music of mine. A particular chorus of a Big Bill Broonzy song comes to mind regarding the need for personal celebrations—especially as it relates to the individuals served. It's entitled, "I Can Do It All By Myself."

I can do it all by myself
I don't need no help
All by myself
All by myself
I don't need nobody helping
I can do it all by myself
I can do it all by myself. [3]

Perhaps an audio CD could be given to each program participant, sort of a statement of each person's desire to create his or her own future.

chapter
seven

So What Is Outcome Management?

"They said you have a blue guitar,
You do not play things as they are."
The man replied, "Things as they are
Are changed on the blue guitar."

—Wallace Stevens

O
UTCOME MANAGEMENT IS A selected leadership course of action that emphasizes a commitment to continuous improvement, exploration, personal responsibility, and learningfulness while emphasizing the importance of all organizational relationships. Everything counts.

The cartoon on the following page reflects a frequent organizational dilemma; there may be a change in the outward appearance of what we do, but the content of our actions remains the same.

Outcome Management is a new way of thinking. It's not just changing the signs and symbols of organizational life. It is an understanding that there are no fixed standards which, once achieved, result in a final outcome. Outcome Management is a journey in a different direction.

Outcome Management is about the pursuit of truth. It demands a total commitment to knowing what's going on—and that is no easy task. Discovering the true value of things in a large organization is one of the greatest challenges that administrators face. In many organizations there is a great reluctance to tell the truth, as well as a great reluctance to hear it. Some-

"You may be a butterfly,
but you still *think* like a caterpillar."

times the routes of communication are so complicated that it takes a very long time for the message to even reach the proper person.

Outcome-oriented organizations will, of necessity, become less hierarchical and more horizontal in structure. Drawing new boxes on the table of organization, or changing the names of the incumbents, won't result in the achievement of outcomes. Moving the boxes on a table of organization won't move an organization—only new ways of thinking can do that.

To succeed in reworking and rethinking the structure of an organization, just as much attention must be given to the white spaces around the boxes as to the boxes themselves. One box that is probably not needed in an outcome-based organization is the one called quality improvement, quality assurance, or quality enhancement. In the new way of thinking this responsibility is found in every box. It cannot be delegated away from daily operations. No one can say, "Quality assurance? Sorry, that's not my department"—it is everyone's responsibility.

An Inclusive Model

Many individuals employed in organizations serving the disabled, whether program staff or management, are increasingly becoming committed to a management approach that emphasizes the achievement of outcomes.

Of concern to me is the growing tendency to see the stuff of outcomes as an alternative to the process orientation of the past. Outcome Management is not a substitute for past approaches. "We no longer need to do professional assessments," an executive director announces, and suddenly documentation and details are no longer important.

Outcome Management is an inclusive model. It incorporates the positive contributions of previous learning, including the recognized value of individualized participant processes.

To follow practices that facilitate outcome achievement is not to reject the valuable elements of previous models. Rather, it is to critically examine the detours and dead-ends encountered while traveling a political or bureaucratic process highway for so many years. All of the past contributions that have helped to improve the lives of persons with disabilities are recognized and examined in the context of today's knowledge.

The paperwork-driven system that prevails today did not develop accidentally. Many of the standards, rules, and performance indicators so rigorously observed today were borne out of the abuses and poor quality of care in the past.

Unfortunately, however, while most organizations improved the quality of their care practices, some did not. Rather than view organizations differently—that is, separate out those who provide excellent services from those who do not—the common bureaucratic tendency is to keep on adding more standards that are applied to every organization.

As a result, program evaluators and inspectors focused on counting how many times a bird flapped its wings—without paying sufficient attention to whether or not the bird could fly.

Outcome Management is about assisting the bird to fly.

The following pages of this book share the results of implementing outcome-based management and leadership.

Some projects currently "in the works" are also shared with the hope that readers engaged in similar pursuits will benefit from these insights and also share their successes with others.

Such efforts are not offered as the best way, but they may provide a better way of doing things for many organizations. Even as these thoughts and insights are shared, their effectiveness and efficiency are being studied by a variety of different work groups at Trinity Services.

Outcome Management is not a process or an end point for any organization. It is, however, a useful approach for those staff members interested in results and who recognize the pivotal role that they play in providing services and supports for people with disabilities.

These pages reflect the current journey of the staff at Trinity Services and the places visited along the way.

chapter eight

Getting Started

"Intellectuals are notably prone to believe that when they have said something, they have done something."

—*James Barber*

HAVING THE AUTHORITY TO implement change is meaningless without a willingness and a desire to change. By the same effect, change is difficult to institute without the authority of top management. This chapter is for those readers who are in a position to implement change.

In ideal circumstances, the chief executive officer coordinates an agency's transformation to an Outcome Management organization. Outcome Management cannot be introduced if the boss merely returns from the conference in Arizona or Orlando with the latest *Seven-Step Package for Organizational Improvement*, gives it to one of his top assistants, and asks that it be implemented.

"Keep me posted," he says. "Let me know if you need any help." The experienced assistant has learned to expect such action and has already begun to gather back the old banners, key chains, and posters before the CEO gets back. Loyal assistants begin to let their team leaders know that they are likely to have their groups reworked and probably renamed in the near future.

Unfortunately, much of the intended change introduced in most organizations is of the name brand, pre-packaged variety.

Although it is most desirable to make the transition to an Outcome Management approach beginning with the chief executive, it is possible to introduce the components of Outcome Management at any level of an organization. The advantage of having top leadership on board will become more obvious as follows.

A basic premise of Outcome Management is that our organizations cannot be or become anything that we ourselves are not willing to be or become.

In my early days at Trinity Services I struggled to get key staff members motivated to worry more about how we presented ourselves to the general public. Quite frankly, the culture was one of *learned helplessness*. Employees were conditioned to feel that nothing they did, or didn't do, would make a difference.[1] It appeared to me that staff members were competing for spots in the snow in which they could lie down and die. Attempting to inspire them and having just seen Tom Peters' video, *A Passion for Excellence*, I sardonically suggested to all of the thirty or so employees that perhaps we could upgrade our letterhead and have as our tag line: *Trinity Services, We're No Worse Than Anyone Else.*

I was, to say the least, concerned, not to mention depressed, when a few employees, thinking I was serious, agreed that this motto sounded pretty good to them.

The beginning point for introducing organizational change—especially Outcome Management—is to create and experience a period of organizational introspection and self-awareness. In this book such efforts cover two primary areas: clinical or programmatic issues and management practices.

From a programmatic perspective, the focused-on issues originated from the question, "How well are we serving the people in our programs?" The primary vehicle for determining the responses and answers to this question came from utilizing the

Outcome Measures of the Accreditation Council for People with Disabilities.

In the management area, such soul-searching leads to an investigation of all key variables or activities: communication practices—both internal and external—decision-making effectiveness, and all relevant employment practices, including the contents of the employee handbook. Compensation systems, organizational structure, job descriptions, and, perhaps most important of all, the nature of all inter- and intra-organizational relationships are also examined.

Other questions of major significance soon emerged: *How large should we become as an organization? What should be our rate of growth? Where should we get our revenue from? Should we become a multipurpose organization and serve a wider range of people?*

There were more questions than answers. Every effort was made to support the process with factual information—reliable dates and accurate numbers. Continual data gathering was essential.

It rapidly became obvious that future practices needed to be different than those of the past. After making a commitment to the Outcome Management components discussed previously, we focused attention on established practices.

It should be noted that the initial commitment to change and the focus of that change began with the top leadership staff of the organization. Focus groups, task teams, surveys, and other vehicles for employee input came later. They were not, however, limited only to the content of the first agenda.

As the key areas for change were identified, they were processed through the format of the strategies suggested in Richard F. Elmore's article, "Backward Mapping: Implementation Research and Policy Decisions."[2] Although this article was written from the perspective of public policy implementation, it provided a helpful tool for ensuring that the desired changes would be implemented once they were decided upon. The leadership group was attempting to avoid the common downfall of organizational life—that good ideas at the top are never implemented as intended once they reach the outer edges of the organizational structure.

The backward-mapping rationale is quite elegant in its simplicity. Once the desired change in function, operation, or application is well thought out and agreed upon, take the concept to the implementation level of the organization and consider the implications and ramifications of the new direction. What are the potential barriers to full implementation? What are the necessary resources?

After struggling with the issues at this level of the organization, the process works backwards to all other levels of the organization until it arrives back at the originating destination—in this instance, the level of top management.

The probability of successful implementation is greatly increased in such a dynamic. A parallel to such an approach can even be utilized within specific programs. One way this can be accomplished is by asking staff members to come together in a relaxed setting and close their eyes, imagining their program under ideal circumstances. What does it look like? Sound like? What are staff persons doing? What are the program participants doing? Ask the team members to share their ideal imaginings. After those who share their mental pictures complete their descriptions, begin a discussion about what prevents this from happening. The work of the group can now be launched. How will they accomplish this desired future? The individual employee description might be audio taped so that they can be referred back to later. Once again, however, the approach has been to work backwards from the end state.

The results of such organizational introspective processes revealed findings that have perhaps been best captured by Charles Handy in his most recent book, *The Age of Paradox.* Handy proposes that for organizations to be viable and remain competitive in the future, they will realize that what brought them success in the past will not bring them success in the future. This concept is a jumping-off point for one of Handy's most instructive models for managing change—the sigmoid curve.

The Sigmoid
Curve

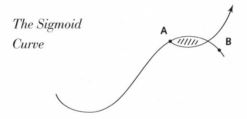

The sigmoid curve is an S-shaped curve that describes the life cycle of a product, the progress of a civilization, the course of a relationship, or the life of an organization. We start out falteringly, cautiously testing the water. Then, if we're lucky (or good), we achieve progressive levels of success. This lasts for so long and, in the end, we decline and perish.

If this were all the sigmoid curve revealed, however, it would be merely depressing. We would simply figure out where on the curve we were and calculate how long we've got left. But, Handy points out that, to manage change and not be swept away by it or see it pass us by, we must know when to start a new curve. Point A is, for some, the pinnacle, a time to rest on laurels and enjoy the success. But our time on the summit of the curve is precisely when we must seek change.

The area represented by the shaded area might very well be described as the place for reflection, dynamic self-awareness, and organizational introspection. Handy further makes the point that if an organization allows itself to reach point B, it will take a Herculean effort to regain or achieve a level of successful performance.[3]

This phase of organizational reflection can be assisted by networking with other organizations, including benchmarking activities. The use of knowledgeable consultants in key organizational areas may also help.

The time spent by each organization in experiencing this process will no doubt vary with personalities of the staff involved as well as the range of complexity within an organization.

It was this period of reflection, discussion, dialogue, and debate that led to the Partnership Agreement mentioned earlier and detailed later in this book.

What must result from this period of deliberation is an agenda of prioritized activities that will be pursued throughout the organization. Once decided upon, the next step is to consider how these desired changes will be communicated throughout the organization.

Rhonda Reger, Loren Gustafson, Samuel DeMarie, and John Mullane provide an excellent model for tackling this next critical stage of organizational transformation in an *Academy of Management Review* article, "Reframing the Organization: Why Implementing Total Quality Is Easier Said than Done." After sharing helpful insights into the fact that employees are immersed in "cognitive framing"—making sense of the events going on around them—the authors suggest a course of action: "The optimal situation for change occurs when the gap between current and ideal is large enough to create the stress necessary for members to desire change, but the dissimilarities are not so great that the ideal is perceived as being unattainable."[4]

Mid-level change is more likely to be successful than incremental change—which might be perceived by employees as fine-tuning or more upward specializing. An incre-

mental approach isn't enough to combat organizational iner-
tia or apathy.

Radical change, what the authors refer to as "synoptic
change," should also be avoided, for such change may appear
too threatening or overpowering.

What constitutes mid-level change will again vary with each
organization. In reality, what may appear as radical change in
one organization may be mid-level in another.

The most desirable situation in presenting desired change,
according to the authors, is to, "Work with those aspects of organizational behavior that are positively aligned with employee
beliefs about the organization's ideal identity."[5]

Because most of Trinity's staff think and feel positively about
the Accreditation Council on Services for People with
Disabilities, especially with regard to the embraced values and
principles and subsequent emphasis on the person served or supported, our management group made the decision to use the
Outcome Measures and the attendant accreditation process as
the vehicle for achieving organizational change.

Management practices that emphasized learningfulness,
Servant Leadership, and relationship building were selected to
accompany the program efforts.

Having gone through a process of self-awareness—which is
never actually completed but occasionally inventoried for con-
versational purposes—and having decided upon the primary
areas of desired change and the manner in which such change
will be implemented, one last dynamic was explored. At Trinity
Services this dynamic is referred to by the question, "Are we getting in the Buick?" Jerry Harvey, author of *The Abilene Paradox*,
is responsible for such a cultural consideration. Dr. Harvey is a
consultant who has been instrumental in shaping Trinity's managerial evolution. Harvey states that, "Organizations frequently
take actions in contradiction to what they really want to do and

therefore defeat the very purposes they are trying to achieve."[6]

"Getting in the Buick" refers to the story Dr. Harvey relates when he, his wife, and her parents agree to drive two hours in an un-air-conditioned 1958 Buick to Abilene, Texas, in the middle of "furnace-like heat" and a dust storm—when no one wanted to go in the first place.[7]

With this context in mind, the question leadership staff asked of each other is, "Are we doing what we really want to do or are we fooling ourselves and each other?"

Knowing that the selected direction was indeed the one we were committed to, the next phase of the transformation process began—communicating this sense of direction to all staff members and interested parties. The primary vehicle used to communicate the change in direction was the face-to-face meeting. At the organization-wide level, the elements were introduced in leadership meetings and included in the agenda of the annual staff retreat. Large meetings were followed up within each program area with smaller team meetings.

The emphasis was on enrolling the staff in the new direction, not on selling them a particular package of new improvements. Enrollment represents membership in a common purpose, a purpose that not only provides organizational meaning but also necessitates commitment and participation. It is a source of employee pride that results in improving the lives of persons with disabilities.

Not all employees enrolled, of course. There are always those who prefer to go their own way and resist the corporate mission. Such individuals, however, are a small minority and tend to select themselves out of the organization over time. Sometimes they receive assistance.

Meetings were augmented by memoranda that clarified the specific goals and time frames. The employee newsletter also underscored the new direction.

Parents and guardians of the individuals served in specific organizational programs were informed of the new direction in a wide variety of meetings, but specifically through program advisory meetings that are held quarterly by each of the major program directors.

The initial informational meetings were soon followed up by specific training events that focused either upon specific program areas or management topics.

Once again the Outcome Measures of the Accreditation Council were used as the primary focal point or lever for making needed program changes. As staff members utilized the Outcome Measures they were encouraged to share their concerns and identify systems shortcomings. Individual departments aggressively pursued the opinions of staff; feedback was also sought through agency-wide committees. Some of the feedback led to the creation of training events in such areas as improving interviewing skills, service planning, and creating a choice-producing environment. Other ideas spurred the formation of ad hoc task groups that included members from across the entire organization.

Specific areas were quickly targeted for improvement or revision, including revision of the Individual Service Plan, revamping of the Personal Record, and standardization of both formats. The number of areas needing improvement was surprisingly large and we soon began prioritizing the work efforts.

The culmination of the work groups and brainstorming sessions resulted in each of the major departments developing its own specific plan of action. The plans were not exhaustive, but laid out the specific goals and intended completion dates for the targeted areas. Each of the department managers was responsible for recording and graphing his or her department's progress. Overall organizational performance was reviewed during the weekly executive committee meetings.

The Issue of Quality

The concept of Outcome Management emerges out of the context of the worldwide concern with quality and total quality management, as well as the revelations of quality control, quality assurance programs, and efforts of quality enhancement.

My interest in quality, however, began in the early 1960s when I was employed as a trucker in a company that manufactured small motors for such appliances as hot air guns, electric can openers, food blenders, and juice extractors. The nature of my work was to deliver specific fasteners and motor parts to the various assembly lines. As time allowed, I would then help move completed motors from the Quality Control department to where they were placed in cardboard cartons and loaded onto delivery trucks.

Two observations regarding quality stay with me even to this day. The first is the manner in which the motors were inspected. No issues of quality were monitored until the motors appeared at the end of the assembly line, labeled "Quality Control." Quality Control consisted of connecting the electrodes to electrical current. If the shaft revolved it was ready for shipment; no attention was paid to determining load bearings or other functions. If the motor ran, it got shipped.

Motors that didn't run were treated in an interesting manner: two gray-haired ladies hit the motors with small hammers and, if that made the motors run, they were stamped "OK" and shipped out. No effort was made to understand why the motor did not run initially. Motors that still did not run were thrown onto a pile to be disassembled.

The worst part came, however, when the motors were loaded into trucks. Four motors were placed in cardboard boxes that seemed to be packed securely. "Do Not Drop" warnings were embellished by "This End Up" instructions printed on all sides of the box. The semi-trailers had to be loaded with as much speed as possible. The drivers' constant badgering prompted the employees on the loading docks to work quickly. Wanting to be valued by my peers and foreman I proceeded to carry several boxes at a time and placed them carefully at the front end of the truck. My co-workers tolerated this behavior for ten or fifteen minutes, at which point one of them told me, "We'll never get this truck loaded if you're going to carry every box that way." Everyone agreed, including the foreman, and so we loaded the truck like it had always been—pick up a box, toss it to the end of the truck, and have someone inside the trailer stack it with the others. No attention was ever paid to the correct manner of loading. I assumed that this practice was acceptable since no one from the front office ever came by and observed the process. Returned motors were unloaded in a similar way—only this time they were tossed off on the loading docks to be loaded onto skids for later disassembly.

Quality as a business concern barely existed, but it certainly was needed. So what is quality in an area much more complicated than the manufacture of small motors?

In providing services to individuals with disabilities, quality is certainly more than one thing. There is no definition of quality that is content-free; a small motor is obviously not the same as what results or occurs during a service transaction.

chapter.
nine

Barriers to Implementation

"It is a funny thing in life, if you refuse to accept anything but the best you often get it."

—*Somerset Maugham*

IN ATTEMPTING TO MOVE toward an organizational management philosophy that emphasizes the importance of achieving outcomes, most organizations will likely encounter some resistance. The nature of the resistance will often occur primarily among the most significant stakeholders, such as managers and professional staff. In other instances, the rank-and-file employees will show reluctance as well.

What follows is a brief description of the major barriers that might be encountered in pursuing an outcome orientation. As you will see, some of the barriers stem from specific structural issues and subsequent organizational processes, others result from belief systems.

Structural Hindrances

In a helpful discussion of the dynamics and interplay of small groups, hierarchy, bureaucracy, and networks, Jessica Lipnack and Jeffrey Stamps, in *The Age of the Network,* provide an excellent understanding of the role these management forms play when they come together in the contemporary organization.[1] This work is very helpful in developing strategies for more effective organizational design.

Too Many Layers

Outcome Management recognizes the positive and perhaps necessary aspects of hierarchy in an organization; it also recognizes the pitfalls. Easy access to organizational members and decentralized availability and decision-making—as well as unencumbered communication practices—are all earmarks of a structure that facilitates the pursuit of organizational, team, and individual outcomes. As fewer and fewer people are allowed to report directly to the CEO, more and more layers must be created to administer the business of the organization. With these additional layers comes greater concern over procedures, regulations, and the impression of front-line employees that they are effectively isolated from top executives.

Many organizational observers believe that the best measure of the effectiveness of an organization's communication system is the speed with which bad news reaches the top. It is likely that in two organizations—each having essentially the same size and purpose—the range in time may reflect a matter of minutes or hours in one, versus days or weeks in another.

David Brown, in *Managing the Large Organization,* provides an excellent analysis of the downside of hierarchy. He considers such elements as the tendency to limit creativity, maintain the status quo, distort communications, and emphasize the chain of command. He explores the problems of lowered employee commitment to organizational purpose, duplication of effort, and outright employee discouragement.[2]

Facilitating the outcomes of the people served or supported is very difficult for certain organizations. By the very nature of their structure, these organizations must spend an inordinate amount of time on processes and procedures meant to accomplish *organizational* outcomes.

Hierarchy as a structural reality is not confined to the large organization. Many small organizations have more levels than are necessary; in some organizations this may be only one unnecessary level, but the negative effect is nevertheless felt throughout the organization. It is unfortunate that many organizational leaders and boards of directors fail to consider this variable while yet trying to implement quality improvement plans.

Size

Although no one has conducted a scientific investigation of the relationship of implementing an Outcome Management approach to organizational size, it seems self-evident that an organization employing 500 people, spread across multiple corporate sites and staggered into three shifts, will have greater difficulty than a single-purpose organization of twenty-five employees at one site. Many more events need mediation in the larger organization. As a result, greater attention must be given to such matters as communication systems, decision-making practices, and employee involvement.

As might be expected, the speed with which larger organizations can adopt different management styles and practices tends to be much slower than their smaller counterparts.

Bureaucratic Boxes

As implied in the discussion of hierarchy, there are benefits from including the positive elements of bureaucratic design in today's organizations. The use of policies and procedures, appropriate specialization of tasks, and delegation of authority are three of the positive manifestations.

Outcome Management, however, cannot be achieved through the addition of boxes, the renaming of boxes, or movement of boxes on an organizational chart. What happens when a new problem or new idea surfaces? If new boxes are drawn, new departments created, and new titles conferred, then the bureaucracy will have to be examined in relation to the desire to proceed differently. Whether or not bureaucracy is a barrier to new ideas can be easily detected in most organizations.

Bureaucracy seems to show up as an unwelcome guest in most organizations, even when invited. As a result, leadership staff must continually worry about the presence of too many departments, too many titles, too much specialization, too much centralization, and too much authority at the top.

Rigid bureaucracies rely on scapegoating as the preferred method of accountability, rather than seeking to understand any underlying systems problems that may be the cause of organizational problems and difficulties. Bureaucratic influences that impede the achievement of organizational outcomes must be scrutinized and eliminated whenever possible.

Job Description and Design

Job design is the fourth aspect of organizational structure that can act as a barrier—specifically, the notion that work can be contained in what is commonly referred to as the "job description." Recently, I reviewed the organizational chart of a medium-sized agency that serves people with disabilities. The organization provided both day and residential services. What I discovered in my review was the presence of more than ninety separate job descriptions.

Having this many individual job descriptions certainly reflects the good intentions of hierarchy and bureaucracy gone awry. What was also interesting was the limiting nature of the job descriptions themselves. The amount of judgment or discretion included in the descriptions varied widely. Some had very little, others had moderate opportunities for self-direction.

None of the descriptions, however, were rich and abundant in terms of independent authority.

Departmentalization, rigid spans of control, and little variation of activity characterized the job descriptions of this organization. These limiting job descriptions resulted in high job dissatisfaction, frequent absenteeism, and, not surprisingly, excessive employee turnover rates. When employees aren't allowed to think for themselves or to use their own judgment, a major barrier to implementing outcome-oriented management systems emerges.

Unhealthy Mindsets

The use or misuse of organizational structure can obviously be a barrier. Other variables, however, also interfere with a new way of thinking and acting. Behaviors, beliefs, and attitudes that inhibit growth, suffocate change, and limit free thinking are mindsets that erect barriers to Outcome Management in an organization's culture.

Only We Have the Truth

This mindset (also known as, "If we didn't think of it first, it can't be any good") is evident in many corporations today.

Standardized assessments, popularly utilized check lists, or published examples of best practices are routinely rejected in those organizations that have "The Truth." The actors in this drama frequently contend that such instruments do not capture their organization's uniqueness. Further inquiry generally reveals the delusion that the staff of this organization serve the most difficult individuals, receive the least funding, and provide services better than anyone else.

We're Already Doing It

It is perhaps obvious that this mindset can closely parallel the thought processes of those who have the truth. Because this mindset can exist independently it is presented separately.

Frequently found in the organizations that share this mindset is a verbal response to any new suggestion or proposal: "We're already doing it." Staff members then go to elaborate measures to convince the idea-maker that he or she is misinformed or uninformed.

When pursuing a course of Outcome Management, those acting as change agents should anticipate this response.

In some instances this response reflects a genuine lack of understanding, in others it reveals a defensiveness, and in still other instances a recognition that something different will be required of the respondent—in this context the something different is probably understood, but still rejected because of the expectation to operate differently.

It's Too Hard

This mindset may stand alone or be accompanied by the companion thought, "We don't have the resources" or "We don't have enough staff."

The question may be asked, "Why should we do this when we can do something easier?" Reluctant managers contend that they can't or won't be able to do what is requested because they just can't get good staff people. If they could only hire college graduates, perhaps then they could do it. But in the meantime, the proposed new behavior or practice is viewed as being unrealistic.

Unfortunately, in some circumstances this mindset also reflects a climate of mistrust. What if the new approach fails? People working in organizations that do not trust their employees know they will be punished for failing. Some employees believe it is better to reject the new pattern of behavior and be seen as reluctant rather than to attempt the new behavior and worry that failure or less than perfect results will lead to organizational retribution.

A variation on this theme sounds a lot like NIMBY (not in my backyard)—in the organizational environment it's expressed as NIMDD (not in my disabilities department). *It's okay in other departments that really need it, but that's not what my department needs. We don't need to focus our attention on outcomes. We need a mission statement, a vision, or perhaps even a People First chapter.*

Weak Management & Leadership

Just as mindsets and structure can prevent acceptance of an Outcome Management system, so can weak management or leadership.

Having the Wrong Person at the Top

For an organization to progress toward a higher regard for outcomes, individuals must be both committed to the new endeavor and knowledgeable as to what must be done to accomplish the objectives of an outcome orientation.

As suggested in the previous chapter, any organizational change is accelerated when the chief executive officer embraces the process. Outcome Management is a top-down process—with the recognition that "top" can mean department head, program manager, team leader, or whomever. The top, according to current management literature, can also mean the center of a sphere of influence. In the future, this centrally-focused model may replace the pyramid of organizational hierarchy. Outcome Management doesn't typically bubble up from the hourly employees working on the front lines, though. These employees may serve as catalysts, and may desire to do things differently, but the changes described in these pages are unlikely to be initiated at this level. Weak leaders and managers often contribute to the generation and spread of corporate politics, which result in turf battles, empire building, and baronial (department head) warfare. Organizations in the midst of internal power struggles will be unable to introduce and execute the work that must be done if an outcome approach is being considered.

The concept of "champion" has recently emerged in the management literature to describe someone who, through both word and deed, does whatever is necessary to accomplish the needed changes. For organizational change to take hold in any significant way, champions must emerge in the workplace.

Some Notions on Emotion

Just as weak managers or leaders are barriers to organizational change, leadership staff who are not emotionally up to the tasks of management are equally damaging.

Managers need to be thermostats and not just thermometers with respect to the temperature of the organizational activities that surround them.

It is not an understatement to contend that managers must first of all keep peace in the valley—but not peace at any price.

Emotional maturity is always required of organizational leaders, but especially in times of proposed change or on journeys of some ambiguity. To proceed when everything is not certain, when there is more gray than black or white, requires a stable constitution.

The emotional behavior of organization leaders may be a more frequent barrier to change than most organizational observers are willing to admit. Better to say there is a breakdown in communication, an unclear mission statement, or a lack of resources than to suggest that some individuals do not function at an acceptable level of emotional maturity.

CLINICAL

ISSUES &

INSIGHTS

chapter
ten

The Service Agreement

"Managers must be aware that friends will do more for each other than strangers."

—*William Glasser, M.D.*

I N CHAPTER THREE, THE IMPORTANCE of developing and maintaining sound and respectful relationships was considered. Employee-to-employee interactions and expectations were emphasized.

This chapter highlights the significance of establishing the same type of relationship with the person served or, if appropriate, the parent, relative, or legal guardian.

In this regard, the pivotal questions to answer are: How will the organization and person seeking services relate to each other? What are the mutual expectations? How will conflict be resolved? Which issues are most important to the organization and which are most important to the person being served?

Determining Treatment & Habilitation Priorities

There are a number of ways of conceptualizing and prioritizing the areas of one's life in which personal improvement is sought. For individuals with disabilities, people working in the field seem to hover around the extremes of a continuum with the first point representing the person's wants, where choice is the governing principle and input from professional staff is subordinate to personal freedom. The second point embodies a focus on needs, where professional expertise is the governing principle and individual choice is subordinate to a professional's knowledge of what is best for the person. An appropriate balance between the two is lacking in many organizations that serve persons with disabilities.

Because staff members frequently seek specific direction in weighing a concern for quality of care with quality of life issues, and struggle to know what particular aspects of a person's life should or could be addressed from an ethical, socially responsible perspective, the following statement of involvement is offered: "Staff of this organization, in addition to assisting the person achieve his or her personal goals and learning objectives, *will address those behaviors that prevent a person from becoming physically or psychologically close to another person.*" It is essential to explicitly state the organization's treatment and habilitation priorities before any services begin. If the guardian or person seeking services does not agree with this philosophical foundation, he or she may pursue services from another provider.

This statement, put another way, says that the organization will direct its resources and energy to enabling a person to become as much a part of the community as he or she desires, without forfeiting professional responsibility during the process. Readers interested in the study of choice and community inclusion may wish to read *Ethical Issues in Developmental Disabilities* by Linda Hayes, Gregory Hayes, Stephen Moore, and Patrick Ghezzi.[1]

It also directs staff persons to such unpleasant areas of life as drooling, incontinence, physical aggression, and self-injurious behavior. Such behaviors represent the required courses for individuals seeking to be served by the organization. They are asked to work on these behaviors. This is not to suggest that the response to such distance-keeping behaviors will be heavy-handed or even addressed first. But, during the course of being enrolled in the service or supports of the organization, such behaviors will be addressed at the right time and place by the right people. The important point is that everyone knows of this expectation from the beginning of service provision. The value expressed in this approach is done without apology: to be human is to be able to be with other people. Treatment or habilitation practices should be worked out with each person served. Just as most people have priorities in their lives—to lose weight, quit smoking, learn how to drive, learn how to type—so is it with people with disabilities. They would like to learn or work on certain skills or behaviors first.

The Service Agreement

The practice of creating a Service Agreement may seem unnecessary or bureaucratic. But it is, in fact, the primary method for building and maintaining relationships, for it makes ambiguous areas explicit and reduces areas of possible contention and disagreement.

Both parties, the staff representing the organization and the person or guardian seeking services, should feel free to raise issues for potential inclusion. This document spells out the organization's resources and philosophy—what it can and cannot do or, for that matter, what it chooses not to do. These matters may cover such issues as staffing levels, participation in fundraising activities, program availability, safety and security, coeducational housing, possession of guns, and communication expectations.

The contract or agreement outlines the expectations in broad areas and might include such elements as:

Organizational Goals

Included here are such issues as the goals of community inclusion, the implementation of specific programs or services, statements of rights, the range of recreation opportunities, and the availability of leisure time activities.

Reporting of Significant Information

The manner in which such issues as accidents, illness, suspected abuse or neglect, or any other significant events are communicated to the guardian are detailed on an individualized basis. The method of handling formal investigations is also spelled out in this section.

Medical Services

Identifying preferred physicians and dentists and other medical specialists occurs in this section. Other areas of concern might include desired hospitalization practices.

Financial Services and Records

The methods used by the organization to accept and use funds is outlined. The nature and frequency of financial reporting is considered, as well as the need for the guardian to provide basic information for any relevant benefit programs such as food stamps, Social Security, public aid, or Medicaid. Decisions regarding the establishment of trust funds or banking accounts are communicated here.

Appeals Process

The methods by which parents and the individuals served can appeal organizational decisions are specified. In many instances, these issues are acknowledged and agreed upon through the receipt of organizational policies or procedures.

Miscellaneous Areas

Important topics not covered elsewhere, such as seeking consent for the release of information, would be included under this heading.

ⁱ

The Service Agreement creates the foundation for subsequent interactions. What neither party wants is surprises. By fully discussing the issues important to both parties and the nature of the expectations that accompany them, the possibility of disappointment and disagreement is minimized. Either of the parties may decide, in the course of developing this agreement, to discontinue or terminate the relationship. This process allows the persons seeking services to make informed decisions about whether or not this is the right organization for them.

Once agreement is reached about the nature of the services or supports to be provided, the next phase of the process begins, the self-assessment interview.

chapter eleven

The Self-Assessment

"Self-respect arises only out of people who play an active role in solving their own life crises... To give people help, while denying them a significant part of the action, contributes nothing to the development of the individual... it is not giving but taking—taking their dignity."

—Saul Alinsky

B EFORE DISCUSSING A NUMBER of issues that are of significance in the treatment or habilitation process, an introductory comment is in order.

Some of the methods or practices I suggest are counter-intuitive. That is, if you only rely on a "gut feelings" or common sense approach in accomplishing your organization's work, the results may be disappointing compared to what could have been accomplished if further exploration had ensued. This point is best illustrated by a discussion of the self-assessment interview.

If you ask the typical staff member, "Who would be the best person to interview someone with disabilities about his or her future plans?" the intuitive, it-feels-right-to-me response would likely be, "the person who knows the individual the best."

In actual practice, however, what frequently happens is that the person conducting the interview—the person who indeed knows the individual better than anyone else—often assumes that he or she already knows what the person will say and does not allow for full thought development or seek to elicit additional information.

Often, staff members draw conclusions based on their familiarity with the person, only to discover the error of their ways when another person, not directly working with the person being served, seeks explanations and understanding and uncovers additional insights that otherwise would not have come to light.

Conclusions regarding choice frequently arise from intuitive error. Linda Hayes, Director of the Behavior Analysis Program at the University of Nevada-Reno, observes: "Asking people what they want is not always an effective procedure for finding out what people truly want... Choosing is affected by the audience present when a choice is made. Significant life choices are often made in the presence of interdisciplinary treatment teams. Under such conditions, we should not be surprised when individuals tell us what we want to hear. This is especially likely when the questions contain the answers, as when a person is asked, 'You do want a job, don't you?' or 'Your new apartment is very nice, isn't it?'"[1]

Hayes also points out other false assumptions when it comes to choice and people with disabilities. Assuming a repertoire of answers in a person who is not experienced or doesn't possess the requisite skills to generate possible alternatives to a question is a mistake. Likewise, believing that a person's activities represent preferences assumes choices which may not exist.[2]

The Individual Self-Assessment

As an organization becomes more outcome-oriented, it is important to examine all of the operating premises and principles of the organization. The results of such efforts lead to the following premise with respect to the desire to provide the highest quality supports and services: the foundation for providing services is the Individual Self-Assessment. All programs or activities, intentions, or suggestions should tie back to this interview and its documentation.

It is not a once-a-year, "I've got to update it" document, but rather a dynamic source of information that is regularly updated and revised as an individual's life changes over time.

The instrument recommended for use is the *Outcome-Based Performance Measures*, published by the Accreditation Council on Services for People with Disabilities. This instrument is favored because it is based on solid research activities. The outcome areas represent the actual life concerns of individuals with disabilities—including people with such diagnoses as mental illness, mental retardation, cerebral palsy, seizures, and autism.

The Self-Assessment is, in many ways, based on the previous standards developed by the Accreditation Council in surveying and reviewing organizations that seek to improve the quality of their services.

The thirty Outcome Measures for individuals with disabilities are presented below.

Outcome Measures for People

Personal Goals	1.	People choose personal goals.
	2.	People realize personal goals.
Choice	3.	People choose where and with whom they live.
	4.	People choose where they work.
	5.	People decide how to use their free time.
	6.	People choose services.
	7.	People choose their daily routine.
Social Inclusion	8.	People participate in the life of the community.
	9.	People interact with other members of the community.
	10.	People perform different social roles.

Relationships	11.	People have friends.
	12.	People remain connected to natural support networks.
	13.	People have intimate relationships.
Rights	14.	People exercise rights.
	15.	People are afforded due process if rights are limited.
	16.	People are free from abuse and neglect.
Dignity & Respect	17.	People are respected.
	18.	People have time, space, and opportunity for privacy.
	19.	People have and keep personal possessions.
	20.	People decide when to share personal information.
Health	21.	People have health care services.
	22.	People have the best possible health.
Environment	23.	People are safe.
	24.	People use their environments.
	25.	People live in integrated environments.
Security	26.	People have economic resources.
	27.	People have insurance to protect their resources.
	28.	People enjoy continuity and security.
Satisfaction	29.	People are satisfied with services.
	30.	People are satisfied with their personal life situations.[3]

After the staff is familiar with the instrument, participates in some role-playing exercises, and discusses how the standards should be used, an appointment for a self-assessment interview is made with the person enrolled in one or more of the organization's programs.

When an individual does not have verbal skills, the recommended course of action is to interview the staff members or persons who know the person best. (Although this is not a perfect solution, methods of directly interviewing non-verbal individuals are being researched.) Family members and direct contact workers frequently know the person better than anyone. As much information as possible should always be sought from the person served.

Do not presume that employees possess the necessary ability to interview people with disabilities, especially individuals who may be more cognitively impaired. One of the discoveries—and there will be many in moving towards an Outcome Management approach to delivering services and supports—is that staff members are often assumed to have the requisite ability when in fact they do not. Organizations desiring to improve their quality of services should pause to examine the interviewing skills of their staff; communication seminars, role-playing, using videotaped interviews, and participating in workshops are helpful in developing confidence and competence.

Because the Self-Assessment is so critical to determining future actions, at least two staff members ought to participate in the interview. There should probably be one person from the residential program and one from the vocational program, if the person served is with the organization on a twenty-four-hour, supervised basis.

During training it may be helpful to have three staff members present (assuming this is not overwhelming to the person being interviewed). The third person observes, sharing his or her insights and observations in a post-assessment meeting. This technique has proven to be very helpful. As mentioned in the introduction, one of the changes made in interviewing program participants occurred as a result of this process. It was initially thought that the person who should conduct the self-assessment interview was the person who knew the individual best—the assumption being that there would be greater freedom to elaborate and greater support. Instead, a tendency to answer for the person was noticed, making conclusions before further inquiry might reveal something different, or assuming that the person meant what the staff member thought he or she meant, based on previous conversations. Staff members who had viewed themselves as the person who knew the program participant best were often surprised by what was shared.

When two staff members participate in the self-assessment process, the result is a richer, more abundant understanding of the person's needs and wants.

The optimal interview should flow naturally and flexibly; the thirty items of the Outcome Measures do not have to be rigidly followed in the order presented. In fact, many staff members prefer to end the interview with a discussion of the person's life goals rather than to begin on that note.

In addition to the questions included or suggested in the pages of the Outcome Measures, staff members presently conducting such interviews also pursue deeper areas of inquiry when contextually appropriate.

Such incisive questions are as follows:

1) What do you want? (stated in positive terms) to be explained by the person interviewed.
2) How will you know when you have it? (What will you see, hear, feel?)
3) Where, when, and with whom do you want it?

4) What will accomplishing this outcome do for you?
5) How will having this outcome affect other aspects of your life?
6) What resources do you already possess that will contribute to getting your outcome?
7) What additional resources do you need in order to reach your outcome?
8) What actions are you taking that will move you toward your outcome? What else could you be doing?[4]

The relevance of these additional questions is perhaps the most obvious when exploring the territory of goal development. Many of these questions are also pertinent in considering the other outcome areas of the Self-Assessment.

Some brief comments regarding question number six, "What resources do you already possess that will contribute to getting your outcome?" are in order. This is a powerful question, not only in terms of the specific, sought-after responses—which may include such responses as friends, specific skills, and financial resources—but because it contextually reinforces for the individual being interviewed, as well as the interviewer, the key realization that most people do have resources. Sometimes they have not recognized them, but most people, including those with substantial disabilities, have resources.

Organizations seeking to improve their functioning and effectiveness should consider the strategy of asking all key management staff to conduct or participate in at least two self-assessment interviews. This includes everyone from the chief executive officer to the director of financial operations to the program chiefs and key support staff. The organization will not be able to stay the same after such an endeavor.

In all probability, many of these staff members may become situationally depressed after conducting interviews.

They recognize that so little meaningful work or planning had occurred previously. This does not mean that the staff members were not working hard or were not committed. It means that they were probably working on the wrong things more often than they realized.

Time for Confession

Following the above suggestions, I participated in several interviews with individuals served by this organization. It was indeed disconcerting to find out that so much of what we were doing was off target and did not relate to what the person served wanted or needed the most.

All of what we did, of course, sounded good and was actually well written. Most of our efforts could be described as being politically and programatically correct. There was not, however, a source document that could be referenced to anchor the staff activities. Our clinical folders and service plans were well organized and could rival anyone's. And there were plenty of goals and objectives, all of which were being diligently charted and carried out. It was embarrassing to realize that we were spending so much of our time and resources on disconnected activities that had little to do with what the person really wanted.

An organization's staff, after participating in such self-assessment interviews, cannot stay the same—nor can the organization. The experience of talking with the people served motivated us to go the next step and examine all of the organization's practices.

One interesting and positive outgrowth of instituting the self-assessment interview was the enthusiasm and support of the parents and family members who participated in the process. The serious nature of the inquiry, combined with the relevance of the information discussed and discovered, was genuinely appreciated.

During one interview, a mother of one of the program participants posed a very thought-provoking question. "What did you do before you started this new process?" Silence prevailed. The honest answer with respect to Self-Assessment was, "Nothing." The closest approximation was the collection of professional assessments found in the individual's chart. These piece-of-the-person observations did not even come close to providing such a meaningful document. This is not to deny the importance of professional assessments.

Now, however, these assessments follow the Self-Assessment when needed, if at all. A Self-Assessment that follows the guidelines of the Accreditation Council necessarily takes the format of a document resembling a journal or biography; it can't be readily computerized with a long list of "yes" or "no" responses followed by the perfunctory string of added on, "individualized" objectives. This new self-assessment process brings the opportunity for the individuals served to answer more than yes or no questions. They, along with staff, will begin to be able to answer open-ended questions.

In general, a self-assessment interview takes from between two and three hours to complete. It may be the most valuable time spent for the individuals served. As previously stated, the content of the document is constantly being revised—at the pace and dictates of the person—as his or her life changes or choices are made. Changes are not made at the fixed intervals specified in a compliance-driven policy or procedure manual.

chapter twelve

The Individual Service Plan

"We find no real satisfaction or happiness in life without obstacles to conquer and goals to achieve."

—*Maxwell Maltz*

THE SERVICE AGREEMENT AND the Self-Assessment lead to the third important document in the services and supports provided to an individual with disabilities by an organization, the Individual Service Plan. This might, in fact be a document entitled "Jane M's Plan for the Future."

In creating a service plan, the dynamics of the relationship, the quality of the interaction, and the richness of the information shared—as well as the commitment to implementation—are much more important than the literary skills of the author. High-sounding plans with superficial understanding and shallow meaning—or poor follow-through—are worthless.

What Should Be Covered?
Background Section

This section of the plan for the future provides the basis or rationale for the Service Plan meeting. Why did all of the people involved come together? Did the individual being served ask for the meeting? Has something significant occurred? Is something significant about to occur? In some states, a regularly scheduled meeting is a regulatory requirement or a condition of receiving funding for the person or the organization.

The People Involved

The individuals present at the meeting generally fall into one of two categories: those close to the person for whom the meeting has been called, and those who are interested or will be involved, even if they do not know the person directly. They are there to contribute their expertise in areas that are relevant to the person served.

Ideally, the individual is assisted to chair his or her own meeting. This is not always possible, however. In such cases the individual should be asked who he or she would like to chair the meeting instead. People often ask a friend to be present. This is often helpful and leads to a more relaxed atmosphere; other close friends or family members might also be invited. Anyone who is close to the person is, with his or her permission, invited to participate. Others present may include therapists, other professionals, and potential treatment collaborators.

Personal Sketch

The Personal Sketch is a unique feature of the Service Plan. It creates a primary location where new or newly involved staff members can learn about the person they are or will be serving in an in-depth, personal way. Nowhere is the importance of using humanizing language as important as it is in this section of the plan. The standard is to describe people as we would like to be described ourselves and as we would want our loved ones described. This section introduces the person served to everybody with whom he or she will interact, with the notion that everything counts. To allow language that is pejorative is to continue to allow less than what we would want for ourselves. As soon as you see a document that begins, "This twenty-five-year-old, Caucasian male…" or something similar, ask the author to consider rewriting it. I recently read one such document and it included the observation that, "Barbara enjoys edibles." Is that how we would choose to describe our husbands or wives? Our children? Is that what she really enjoys—edibles? Probably not. A useful learning exercise is to ask such individuals as qualified mental retardation professionals (QMRPs) and others to write brief descriptions of each other. It sensitizes them. Another fun option is to ask these same staff members to write a brief description of their executive director, knowing that they will share it with him or her. Employees who author these documents benefit from trading their efforts with colleagues and reviewing each other's descriptions.

This section of the document provides helpful insights and observations that assist staff members in creating a mental image of the person. They could, after reading the material, pick the person out of a crowd. Readers would know something of his appearance, how he presents himself to the world. They could tell someone else about his interests and hobbies—perhaps he has a favorite expression or style of clothing.

One of our staff members recently reviewed a note from a parent stating that she had mailed a copy of her son's plan to her other children who lived out of state, because she said it so accurately captured who her son and their brother was.

The following example reflects the desired approach:

Personal Sketch

George Davis [not real name] is a tall (about six feet), middle-aged man whose beard and hair are distinctly gray.

Given that he walks several miles each day, it is no wonder that he stays in good shape and as he says, "Keeps the fat off." Except for glasses (he's nearsighted) and a slight limp of his right leg, he is in good health.

George enjoys talking and being with people. Not being able to read or write does not prevent him from making friends or participating in many community activities, including going to St. Benedict's Church each Sunday or to the YMCA at least two nights a week.

Although he likes being with friends and living with three other people in their small home in Joliet, George also enjoys his privacy and watching television late into the evening in his bedroom. He prefers "M*A*S*H" reruns to Jay Leno and David Letterman.

George has an uncanny ability to recognize the make of cars while they pass along on the street. "There goes a Chevy, there goes a Buick, there goes a Ford," takes on a clear meaning for him. He knows his cars.

Because of his fondness for cars, the staff of Trinity Services' developmental training program is working to help George find a job in which he can work with cars in some way. Job satisfaction is very important to George; he has quit all of his previous part-time jobs.

Although George has many friends, he spends most of his free time with one of his roommates, Ben Archer. They frequently go out to eat at Red Lobster—their favorite restaurant—and to St. Francis College's baseball, football, and basketball games.

George has reported that, if he won the lottery, he would hire a chauffeur, buy a van, and move to Florida. The van would be blue, his favorite color. His favorite possession, which he eagerly shows to visitors, is an autographed picture of Doris Day.

At this time, the most important concern in George's life seems to be the health of his brother, Raymond. Raymond has recently been hospitalized for chemotherapy treatments during the past year.

Personal Values

This is one of the most difficult areas of consideration because it is so often not discussed and many times overlooked. Values may be difficult to discern with a person who is non-verbal and substantially disabled. Once again the effort is to know the person on more than a superficial level. To learn about the meaningful aspects of an individual's life requires that staff members spend time with the person. Is the person religious? If so, to what extent? What is the place of privacy in the person's life? Is he conservative or liberal in his beliefs? What matters the most to this person?

Another discovery made in moving towards an outcome-based management philosophy is the unpleasant realization of how little time is spent by staff members alone with one of the individuals served. Since group activities are the order of the day, it is no wonder that this area comes up short.

The Feeling Spectrum

What makes this person angry or depressed? What causes her to be uncomfortable? What brings happiness and joy to the person? What deep emotions does she express? This section strives to bring a person's emotions, hopes, fears, and passions into consideration.

What is *not* wanted in this section is a computer-generated reinforcer list or a history of likes and dislikes that can range from apples, candy bars, and M&Ms to rock music to favorite TV rograms to visiting the zoo. Generally, such mindless lists are made up of tangible, easy-to-get or offer items. Unfortunately, the influence of such variables as special friendships or creative energies is rarely included within such lists.

Likes and dislikes are important, but the challenge is to dig deeper or reach higher and discover the most significant as well as the less significant emotional factors of a person's life.

Communications

In this section, the person's verbal and non-verbal communications abilities are discussed. Does the person grasp things more easily when they are presented pictorially rather than verbally? Does the person speak a second language? If so, which does he or she prefer?

The use of communication boards or other technological devices should be included in this section.

What Is New or Different?

New and different activities need to be encountered for a person to experience a full life. This section should not only reflect present activities, but what is planned for the future. Visiting new places, seeing new sights, tasting new foods, and meeting new people are all experiences that enable a person to increase his or her ability to make choices. It is not a choice to choose the only experience one has ever had.

Choice, within the field of disabilities, is a frequently misused concept. A parent who states that her daughter wishes to reside in a state institution "because she chooses to" doesn't understand the essence of choice. How could a person who has lived in an institution for twenty-five years know of other alternatives—especially when she never leaves the campus except to go bowling or to the day program? The advocate who contends that an individual can engage in obviously dangerous practices (especially when the person does not understand the consequences) likewise doesn't understand choice. Someone who allows a person to engage in unsafe sexual practices, to skip his medications, to refrain from bathing, or to live in a filthy environment because, "that's his choice," is unclear on the concept. What happens in many public forums on disabilities regarding public policy issues is that obvious disagreements and, in some instances, major conflicts are avoided through a retreat to, "I guess everyone has to make his or her own choices." Choice as a concept is of course never defined, but frequently over-romanticized as a mechanism for resolving disputes. It resembles many union-management agreements in which both parties agree to ambiguous contractual language, assuming that subsequent maneuvering will ensure that the meanings and definitions they hold will prevail.

The point is that we must emphasize the importance of exposing people with disabilities to new experiences in an organized and thoughtful manner.

Creating the Future

The last element of the Service Plan confronts the questions: "What does the person want for the future?" and "How does he or she envision this preferred future?" This is where the issue of needs and wants comes together. It includes statements of goals and objectives.

If the Service Plans for the people you are serving or supporting conclude with a litany of "wills," consider rethinking the intent of this approach. Reading through such a listing, it is not uncommon to find:

- Steve *will* wash his hands after using the bathroom and before meals for three consecutive data collection sessions by January 1, 1996.
- Steve *will* be able to identify the name and value of coins such as quarters, dimes, nickels, and pennies by January 1, 1996.
- Debbie *will* correctly and independently spell the names of all her family members by May 1, 1996.
- Debbie *will* use the computer to type a short letter by May 1, 1996.

To me, these sound more like the demands of an obedience school or a compliant person factory than the desires of someone planning for the future. Objectives like these can be expressed in a more positive way by indicating what the person's long-term goals are and then describing, from the individual's voice, the objectives needed to reach those goals:

> "I want to be able to handle the money I earn from my job. I would like to be able to buy things at the store by myself and to keep a bank account. Being able to manage my own money will make me more independent and I won't have to rely on other people all the time. I agree that the first step in achieving this goal should be learning how to tell the difference between quarters, dimes, nickels, and pennies and their value. I have agreed to try and accomplish this goal for myself."

These kinds of statements flow out of the personal outcomes identified in the self-assessment interview and the Service Plan meeting. Objectives are related to long-term goals and they are stated as outcomes people want to achieve. With this format, objectives that are not part of a person's goals for the future cannot creep into the plan. The objectives are chosen and defined by the individual, not the organization or the family. Each of the objectives should also include a meaningful statement of criteria, so the person and staff will know when he or she has mastered a skill or acquired some knowledge.

It is important to point out that, even in cases in which a person is non-verbal or unable to write, personal objectives can still be identified as they are in the self-assessment interview:

> Debbie's personal goal is to learn how to read and write at a proficient level. She believes that achieving this goal will help her to gain control over her environment by expressing herself in the presence of family and friends, and enlighten others of her potential for personal growth. To achieve this goal, Debbie would first like to learn how to spell. She is extremely close to her family and wants to surprise them by spelling all of their

names. Therefore, Debbie has set the goal of learning to independently spell her family's names.

Such statements of intent, expressed by the individuals in
active terms, shape and reinforce a culture of people's decisions
coming first.

Implementation strategies follow a person's goals and objectives for the future—how will the person and the staff accomplish the objectives?

Implementation Strategy

This nuts-and-bolts section of the record indicates the specific manner in which the goals, wants, and needs—revealed and
identified in the Individual Self-Assessment—are carried out.

Specific information with respect to the who, what, where,
when, why, and how of specific activities is outlined. For example, residential and day program staff members should know
and be able to reference how they are working together to
accomplish the intended results. Progress is recorded and
changes are made as indicated and appropriate.

The actual strategies for implementation are found in the
individual's program book. This is the reference workbook that
includes, among other things, the objectives, criteria, specific
dates, intervention strategies, data collection methods, service
notes, and data sheets to document progress.

∽

In concluding the Individual Service Plan, there are two
other areas that may be necessary to reference. Whether these
matters are included or not depends on each person:

Additional Services & Supports

The kinds of services outlined in this section include those
objectives traditionally defined as service objectives. Helping the

person to obtain food stamps, to apply for other relevant entitlement programs, and making and keeping medical appointments are part of the intent of this section.

Other Interests & Activities

Data collection, as discussed earlier, is a critical method for determining the progress made toward an outcome. People pursue other activities, however, in which they explore and learn informally. In these cases, no data is recorded. Learning occurs incidentally, without the need for data collection. It is essential that these areas be identified. An individual may want to cook, for example. So the person would be included in the kitchen activities and meal preparation because it is important to him or her. Collecting data may not be appropriate—it may even be disruptive—but the person is participating in a meaningful activity that should be recognized for its learning value.

This section concludes the Individual Service Plan. All of the essential elements are accounted for in a readable document that is available to those relevant parties working with the program participant. The person for whom the plan is being designed does, of course, get the first copy.

The specific information regarding the learning techniques to be utilized, time frames, and so forth are found in the Personal Record which will be outlined in the next chapter.

The last item of business in creating a Service Plan is to sign the Statement of Understanding. This is a mutual covenant agreed to by not only the person planning his or her future, but also the representatives of the organization present who will provide the leadership in securing the necessary supports and services in carrying out the plan.

A Brief Note Regarding Signatures

Some individuals may not be able to sign their names or

make an identifiable mark on the document indicating their approval. On an individual basis, thought might be given to having a signature stamp made for each person who needs one. There are several alternatives in developing this possibility:

1) Have two or three staff members write the person's name and allow the person to choose the signature he or she likes best.
2) Guide the person's hand in writing his or her name.
3) Have the person place his or her hand on a staff member's hand and write his or her name.

These options have proven to provide a valuable experience to many people with disabilities. The stamp is kept in their possession and becomes a powerful symbol of independence.

chapter thirteen

The Personal Record

"...There is the place I am in now, where I look back and look ahead, and dream and wonder."

—*Carl Sandburg*
"Between Worlds"

T HE WORK OF PROVIDING supports and treatment, habilitation, or rehabilitation services is gathered and maintained in three key written documents; the Service Agreement, the Self-Assessment, and the Service Plan.

All of these documents are dynamic and should be changed or updated as circumstances dictate. They are not annual compliance documents. These three documents, together with other essential information, are maintained in the Personal Record.

The Personal Record

This document holds the critical information for individuals enrolled in organizational programs. The complexity and comprehensiveness of such records varies with the scope of the services provided. Vital to daily operations, this document may be integral to funding and regulatory bodies as well as to certification or accreditation reviews. The legal requirements with respect to content, confidentiality, and time of retention vary from state to state.

The following section outlines the elements of a Personal Record that reflects an Outcome Management orientation. This emphasis is embodied in both the content selected and in the manner in which such information is recorded and organized.

The Service Agreement sets the stage for the relationship that a participant will have with the organization, and is primarily administrative in nature; the Self-Assessment is the ongoing reference document for all staff members involved in supporting and providing services to a person; and the Service Plan outlines the basis and strategies for goal accomplishment. The Personal Record includes all of the information required by law, as well as the relevant data, important to a full understanding of a person's life circumstances, including service and support resources.

The Personal Record reflects the organization's formal compilation of all key documents.

Identifying Information

This section of the record includes all of the facts and figures that may be required in providing supports or services. Such issues as physical characteristics, social networks, financial resources, and legal status are listed here. It is important to reduce the common redundancies found in most records. Having all the key facts and figures in one location reduces the likelihood of errors and minimizes unnecessary paperwork.

This portion of the record should also include a photograph of the person. This should not be a "mug shot" that looks like the picture on a criminal's rap sheet, but a photograph chosen by the person and taken in a natural setting. Having such a photograph not only emphasizes the personal nature of the record, but enables the organization to describe the person to others in an emergency.

The Individual Service Plan

The Individual Service Plan is available in all program environments since it is the document that directs the daily interactions with the person being served. The master copy, however, is retained in the Personal Record.

When a person is served on a twenty-four-hour basis, the Personal Record is usually maintained in the residential area. There is only one "official" record that integrates key information. Working copies of such sections as the Individual Self-Assessment, however, are available as needed or requested.

Self-Improvement

This feature of the personal planning process is not found in the Service Plan, but is included in the Personal Record. It encompasses many other important aspects of living. This category of concern is not a routine element found in every person's file. Rather, it includes relevant information and the unique areas that a person may wish to experience or change. It also highlights recent accomplishments.

Consider one's physical appearance, for example: "How do you feel about the way you physically present yourself to the world?" For some reason, this question is very rarely asked when talking to people with disabilities. It is readily apparent that many people in our society are concerned with this issue—aerobic classes, diets, health stores, and beauty salons abound. It would seem obvious that people with disabilities might have similar concerns. So why isn't this issue addressed? Why is it so frequently overlooked? The worst-scenario response is that such matters are not a part of our awareness. People with disabilities are different from us. In other instances the challenge to help some individuals in this area may seem too great.

Recently, I interviewed one of our program participants and, as I concluded the self-assessment, I asked, "Is there anything else you would like to talk about?" She began to cry. After regaining her composure, she told me that she did not like the way she looked. She went on to say that her hairstyle bothered her, but she couldn't afford to "have it fixed." On top of that, all of her clothes were old and out of style. She believed that people made fun of her and thought that she wasn't very pretty. As a result of this discussion, a staff member went shopping with her for new clothes, accessories, and make-up. She went to a beauty salon and had her hair cut and styled.

When I saw her a few weeks later she was beaming. She felt more comfortable with her appearance and was confident about going to job interviews and finding a job. Her perspective on the world was different; there was no crying now, only smiles of improved self-esteem.

Not all matters can be addressed as easily, but we have a responsibility to assist those individuals who struggle with these kinds of issues. Not talking about difficult problems won't solve them.

I should point out that the topic of appearance is not explicitly found in the Outcome Measures. Revealing such issues takes probing and patience.

Another feature of the Self-Improvement section of the Personal Record deals with problematic behavior and suggests a different way of looking at the traditional "behavior plan." This approach doesn't dodge the fact that many people—not just people with disabilities—engage in aggressive or seemingly unwarranted behaviors. Instead, it reframes the subject in a more appropriate and scientifically acceptable manner.

Everything a person does represents a behavioral response— the good as well as the bad behaviors. So why have professionals in the field of disabilities decided that "challenging" behaviors warrant a formal behavior plan, while no such behavior plans exist for developing desirable behaviors?

I don't know the answer to this question. But the consequences of this way of thinking have haunted me for many years. For many people with disabilities, their virtual identity and reputation are established by what we don't want them to do. As a result, staff members spend an inordinate amount of time concentrating on what should happen less and less, as opposed to what should happen more and more. The troubling consequence of this course of action is that we abandon the person once we stop his or her behavior.

The approach Trinity is pursuing, with the help of Linda Hayes and her colleagues at the University of Nevada-Reno, is to understand that negative or undesirable behavior is just one part of a person's life. It is not the sum and whole of who the person is. The subsequent intent, then, is to not highlight the negative *over* the positive.

In regard to emphasizing the negative, Linda Hayes writes: "We tend to dichotomize things, the good behaviors and the bad behaviors. Things to produce and things to get rid of. This way of thinking might be alright if it led to an equal distribution of our energies in dealing with production or construction of repertoires as with limiting aspects of them. It doesn't often happen this way, though. Instead, we tend to focus on getting rid of the bad things. So we design procedures to decrease running from the room, to stop aggression, to extinguish pestering. When we are all done the person won't be doing anything, and the plan will have been accomplished."[1]

With this understanding in mind, Trinity discontinued its use of behavior plans and regards "bad behaviors" as areas in need of self-improvement—much like those of you who are trying to swear less or quit biting your fingernails. Now, at Trinity, behaviors previously considered to be the stuff of behavior plans are recognized as areas appropriate for social transition. So it is within this heading that the target behavior is discussed and addressed.

Medication History, Medical Concerns

This section of the record includes the information that has a bearing on a person's health and physical condition.

A medication history is maintained as well as such information, if appropriate, as Tardive Dyskinesia screenings and blood level determinations.

Assessment Summaries

The Self-Assessment is the primary tool for understanding the needs and desires of the person being served. For some individuals this may be the only assessment needed. For others, however, this section may include legally-required assessments that are to be completed on a time-specified basis.

The range of assessments might include speech, vision and hearing, occupational or physical therapy, adaptive behavior, nutritional and psychological health, and others.

A financial assessment may also be found in this section of the record.

Administrative/Legal

This portion of the record includes the Service Agreement, all necessary legal documents, consents for release of information, and copies of guardianship papers, if relevant.

Service entitlements, financial information and other related documents are filed here.

Correspondence

Maintained in this last section are copies of the correspondence received from the organizations that have a service or support impact. Correspondence from family or guardians and other organizations involved in providing services are included.

Personal correspondence received by the person being served is not collected or filed.

chapter fourteen

Outcome Evaluation

"If you don't know where you're going, you will probably end up somewhere else."

—*Laurence J. Peter*

KEEPING STAFF AND MANAGEMENT from straying or leaking, ensuring that programs fulfill their original intents, and, above all, that outcomes are being achieved for the individuals served and supported means establishing a system of checks and balances that accurately assess their success or failure.

Programs could not meet the needs of the people they're designed to assist without the contributions of concerned staff members, parents, academics, and the program participants themselves. Programs for habilitation and skill development must be dynamic and flexible. The scrutiny and judgment of these involved parties is critical to the success of the services that are provided.

The following practices, which Trinity has used successfully, facilitate the process of continuous improvement within the clinical service and support areas.

Program Advisory Committee

Every organization that provides services or supports to individuals with disabilities should have a Program Advisory

Committee. In organizations that operate multiple programs, it may be useful to have several advisory groups, specific to such areas as vocational, children's, and residential programs. These advisory groups should exist not only for reasons of customer satisfaction, but also to provide a needed sounding board for program managers.

In a day of many competing time demands, it may be advisable to schedule such meetings quarterly. The members of the advisory group should be familiar with the program and be able to visit and interact with the individuals served and the employees working within the program.

Opportunities, as well as problems and concerns, should be discussed. Follow-through will determine credibility and future participation. When possible, one or more representatives of the program participants should also be included.

Program advisory groups, besides serving as a vital quality improvement mechanism for the organization, provide a forum for solving organizational problems at the most immediate level of importance.

Program Evaluation

Outcome Management strives to provide the best possible individualized services to each program participant. Satisfaction on a personal basis is secured through the self-assessment process.

It is also important, however, for an organization to take stock of the effectiveness of each program operated. Each program should aim to achieve goals and objectives that are, at a minimum, reviewed semi-annually. Such goals should reflect the progress made toward common goals and objectives indicated in the Individual Service Plans.

Outcomes should result from correct processes. It is essential to carefully define and redefine such processes through analysis and evaluation. This is especially important if services are provided on a small group basis. Most organizations are not able to provide one-to-one services when serving large numbers of people. Some services, such as job coaching, may be carried out in this manner, but in instances of developmental training, day care, or workshop environments, the reality is that individuals will usually be served in small groups. How well those small groups do can be determined by program evaluation. Are the learning and teaching techniques being used leading to the desired outcomes?

It is impossible to answer this question without measuring. What characteristics are evident before, during, and after the measurement? Is data gathered frequently enough to self-correct? Does the staff person conducting such groups have the necessary skills to carry out the stated intent? Have the staff members leaked? Have they strayed from the standard? These questions must be answered continually.

Customer Satisfaction

Several feedback mechanisms are created by an Outcome Management orientation, including the Self-Assessment and program advisory groups.

Another mechanism that helps ensure that outcomes will be achieved is a formal survey of the families, friends, and relatives of the person served. This augments the information received from the program participants themselves. In some organizations, based on the individuals served, the survey may go out to everyone or only to a sample of the potential respondents.

During one month of the year, an organization should mail out a brief customer survey that seeks input across key areas of service or support activity.

Some suggestions regarding this process include:

- Create an instrument that is used with a wide range of

staff and program participant input.
- Do not wait until the ideal one is created to use such an approach. The instrument can be refined every year.
- Gather the returned surveys centrally.
- If there are instances of obvious urgency among the returned surveys, respond individually to the concerns as quickly as possible.
- Review the returned surveys for systems problems within the organization, not for answers to the question: "Who's to blame?"
- Communicate the findings in a manner appropriate to the organization. This might include annual meetings to review the findings. Track the key areas for improvement.
- If it is appropriate to the organization and consistent with the present culture and practices, it might be useful to include a number of Compliment/Complaint forms that could be used during the course of the year by those receiving the quality questionnaires.

With respect to customer satisfaction, all customer complaints should be recorded—across all environments. Such feedback should be gathered on a program-by-program basis and reviewed monthly by the appropriate leadership staff. The nature of the complaints should be graphed for ease of communication, then reviewed by the relevant program advisory groups.

The Listening Ear

The attempt to provide the best services possible can be augmented through other support mechanisms. "The Listening Ear," for example, is a forum for individual complaints and concerns that originated from staff suggestions made during an internal staff development seminar.

This program enables program participants who can use a telephone to report problems or complaints to someone outside of their program. A twenty-four-hour answering machine receives the messages which are responded to immediately. It is an additional and important safeguard against abuse and neglect.

In using this feedback mechanism, the responsibility for receiving and responding to the messages belongs to the chairperson of Trinity's Human Rights Committee. Responses to the messages range from direct follow-up to involvement on the part of program staff who are responsible for the area of concern.

Each person involved in the organization's programs receives a wallet-sized card that belongs to them personally. The program participants are informed of the purpose and proper use of the card in small groups throughout the organization.

Distribution of Employee Handbook

One other suggested practice, which should prove beneficial in providing quality services, is to make the employee handbook available to the individuals served. Recognizing that some, if not many, of the people enrolled in organizations serving the disabled may not be able to fully comprehend the contents, this handbook may also be offered to guardians or involved family members. Distribution of the handbook could occur when the Service Agreement is finalized, during the organization's evaluation month, or at key meetings throughout the year. The reasons for distributing it should be included in the contents section of the employee handbook. Expectations for staff should not be kept secret.

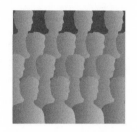

ISSUES OF

MANAGE

MENT

chapter fifteen

Producing Quality

"As an organization grows it must be more human, not less."
—*Swift and Co.*
circa 1970

Q UESTS FOR QUALITY, LIKE quests for the holy grail, tend to begin with much excitement and energy and then bog down in the swamps and deserts of detail. Quality, in the context of organizational dynamics, means excellence of process and outcome. It means that everyone performs to the best of his or her abilities and, more important, that the *system* performs at *its* highest capacity. This ability to employ systems thinking is lacking in managers who may be expert at managing the details, but often are incapable of seeing the forest as anything but a bunch of trees.

Quality does not mean, however, that everything and everyone are perfect. As with outcomes, quality is a journey. Perfection is the destination, but—and this is essential for the organization to realize—it is a destination it will never reach. Employees must strive for excellence and, at the same time, live with the fact that they can't be perfect. An excellent employee is motivated by getting better, as an individual and as a part of the organization.

Essential to an attitude of self-improvement are values. What is the organization trying to accomplish? What is its vision? Without a focus on the mission—and a recognition that daily activities affect outcomes—employees quickly immerse themselves in detail work until they begin asking themselves questions like, "What's it all about?" "Why bother?" or, as Doris Day would ask, "Is that all there is?" Management consultants call this burnout. I call it a loss of values.

Values guide systems. And systems work to fulfill our values. Quality is unattainable in organizations that ignore the relationships between individuals and systems and the ability of individuals to affect those systems. We as managers, then, are responsible for managing systems, values, *and* individuals.

Elliot Jaques, in *Requisite Organization*, explains that successively higher levels of management in an organizational hierarchy must handle progressively longer time periods and greater complexity.[1] This means that managers should be able to anticipate the needs of their subordinates. This kind of foresight isn't possible if managers don't even know what their employees' present needs are.

Servant Leadership

In *The Journey to the East*, Herman Hesse writes about a band of men who set out on a mythical journey. Accompanying them is a servant, Leo, who performs their menial chores, but who also sustains and guides them with his spirit, wisdom, and extraordinary presence. One day Leo disappears and leaves the group in disarray—they cannot go on without him and eventually disband.

Years later, the narrator, one of the original group, stumbles upon Leo. He is taken to the Order that once sponsored their group . We discover that Leo, who had been servant to the party, is the spiritual head of the Order, a great and revered leader.[2]

This paradox was the basis for Robert Greenleaf's work in developing the concept and practice of Servant Leadership. The premise that a leader must first serve those whom he or she would lead and would naturally want to be servant first contrasts sharply with the notion of leadership as being equivalent to authority or privilege, or as a reward for physical, intellectual, or moral superiority. Greenleaf writes in *Servant Leadership*:

> A new moral principle is emerging which holds that the only authority deserving one's allegiance is that which is freely and knowingly granted by the led to the leader in response to, and in proportion to, the clearly evident servant stature of the leader. Those who choose to follow this principle will not casually accept the authority of existing institutions. *Rather, they will freely respond only to individuals who are chosen as leaders because they are proven and trusted as servants.*[3]

With the advancement of computer technology and a new economy dominated by small businesses, employees are asked to know and do more than ever before. The same is true of business leaders. Push-button, top-down management is becoming a relic of the past. Managers are being asked to lead. But, far too many managers are unwilling or unable to serve.

European business guru Jan Carlzon's well-known homily on management is, "If you're not serving the customer, you had better be serving someone who is." Carlzon sums up the most important goal of a manager (or, indeed, anyone) in any organization in a few words. Whether you work in a government agency, a health-care facility, a not-for-profit or for-profit human service agency, you have customers, people without whom your endeavor has no purpose. In any organization, the most critical transactions occur between customers and the people who come in direct contact with them. Thus, Carlzon says, our most essential function is to help the people who help the customers.

As a manager whose job is to serve your subordinates then, ask yourself some tough questions:

Do you persuade? Or do you coerce?
Do you encourage? Or do you order?
Do you offer help? Or do you expect to be helped?
Do you respond to the complaints of workers? Or do you
complain about them?
Do you reward? Or do you take credit?

These questions strike at the paradox of what it means to be a servant leader. The traditional image of the leader is of taking charge, giving orders, and wielding power. Leaders do and should have power. But, if the meaning of power is misguided by tradition, it may be used for the wrong reasons and for the wrong outcomes. Servant Leadership strives to put power into the hands of those being led—a revolutionary notion—but one that is necessary to improve the lives of the members of an organization, a business, or a society.

Putting Servant Leadership into practice is a noble goal, one that takes effort and determination. It contradicts our organizational training and years of relationships with superiors in which it was clear who was supposed to serve whom. Making Servant Leadership work requires a concern for serving the organization's employees and listening to their needs and problems, even though you're the one with the office, the title, and the secretary. It means being like Leo—not only a humble servant, but an inspiring motivator and leader, an indispensable team captain.

At Trinity Services, Servant Leadership is central to the management philosophy. Only one or two layers of organizational structure separate the direct contact workers from the program directors. Communication is facilitated by frequent feedback on employee performance as well as opportunities for employees to give feedback on management's performance. Communication is not curtailed by a pecking order that censures talking to your boss's boss as, "going over your boss's head." The "proper channels" hinder an effective workplace more often than not.

Trinity is by no means an ideal model of Servant Leadership, but no manager asks an employee to do something he or she isn't willing to do. Although Trinity has titles and hierarchies, there is a healthy blurring of individual responsibilities. An employee is more likely to ask, "What do I need to do?" than, "Is it really my job to do that?" Employees and managers who are working toward the same goal often perform work that isn't in their job descriptions. They are more willing to serve and thus, more prepared to lead. The ideal may never be achieved, but the philosophy of Servant Leadership is always with them.

Quality Is Integral

The chapters that follow describe various ideas and programs designed to enhance the ability to implement outcomes in an organization. They are separated as a matter of order and as a favor to the reader. But it is important to understand that they are not separate. Just as quality is integral to every aspect of an organization—you don't strive for quality in some programs and not in others—so is every program integral to achieving quality. If one program doesn't produce quality outcomes, then it affects the level of quality throughout every other program in your organization.

All of the programs and concepts that follow are practiced at Trinity. They are included because they are essential to producing outcomes and because they are inseparable. The relationship between learning and risk-taking is just as complementary as between recognition and partnership—or between quality and learning. Programs cannot flourish in isolation, they must complement and accommodate each another; they must take nourishment from and feed the entire organization.

chapter sixteen

A Learning Organization

"Imagine an organization in which everyone from top to bottom is either actually or potentially learning for the improvement of the organization…"
—*Peter Kline & Bernard Saunders*

JUST AS GOOD MANAGERS and good employees continually strive to improve themselves and their organizations, so they are continually seeking to learn more. The idea that life should be a perpetual process of learning is not a new one, but it does come as a shock to many employees and quite a few managers.

Similarly, the assertion that learning is an inherently enjoyable and even fun experience may be met with skepticism. "If learning is so much fun, why was I so miserable in high school?" an employee may justly ask. To counter this argument I might point out that it was school that was unenjoyable, not learning. In fact, if you think about the people who hated school the most, they were probably also the people who were learning the least. But, whether it is the schools who are to blame for their dread of learning, their parents, or their environments is irrelevant by the time you hire them.

For learning to be embraced by an organization, top management must accept the premise that everyone wants to learn and that everyone is capable of learning. Unlike schools, organizations are compelled to be educators. An organization cannot afford to look forward to the day when they pass their problems on to someone else. Employees will never graduate. They may drop out or you may have to expel them, but along the way, the ones that flounder will drag the organization down with them. An organization cannot be committed to continual improvement without also being committed to continual learning. Helping employees to learn, especially those employees who found school difficult, takes some creativity—along with the realization that the traditional methods used in our schools may not be enough.

The issue of employee learning is always on my mind. Whenever I walk through a program site or observe an employee-to-program participant interaction, the quality of that exchange is a matter of concern.

The consequences of non-trained, poorly-trained, or insufficiently-trained employees is and should be a major concern of all managers. It is not an exaggeration or cliché to say that such concerns may be matters of life and death for the people served. Additional problems crop up—wasted resources, dissatisfied customers, goal displacement, and other general inefficiencies.

Recently, I had an experience that illustrated this concern in a very frustrating way. Needing a new battery for my pickup truck, I headed to one of those big warehouse stores (that shall remain nameless). Once there, I made my way to the battery section, and the dance began.

Because my truck is old, I wasn't sure what cranking amperage it needed. Finding no clerks interested in batteries, nor any customers loitering in the parts department, I thought I could find the answer to my question by myself.

So I went through the computerized battery sales program. Unfortunately, none of the recommended numbers for identifying the correct battery corresponded with the available batteries stacked five feet high in front of me. I was in a hurry.

Desperation sank in, so I went to the customer service area. The manager called the store battery expert over the intercom. Sad to say, he was on his break—but another "associate" would be right there to help me.

Malicious thoughts appeared in my mind as I walked back to the battery display area. A few minutes later, a friendly associate joined me. I told him of my problems and added that I had lost my owner's manual. "What battery should I buy?" I asked. He walked over to the computerized display and hit a few buttons. After complaining that no one had told him how to use this machine, he soon reached the same conclusion I had reached fifteen minutes earlier. The numbers on the screen did not correspond to the numbers on the batteries that were available.

He looked helpless, and for a few moments my malicious thoughts subsided. "That's the trouble with this place," he said, "they don't teach you anything useful." After a few minutes of thought, he had an idea. (There is no denying that he was committed to customer satisfaction.) "Wait here," he said, "I'll be right back." In a few minutes, he returned with a stock boy he found in the back of the warehouse. I led them back to the computer when they returned.

The stock boy (probably not an "associate" because he wasn't wearing a colored vest) strode confidently over to the computerized terminal and hit the OFF button. "That won't help you," he said.

Intrigued by his insight, I told him of my need to replace the dead battery in my truck. By now I had crawled through the battery piles and had found two "purchasing your new battery" booklets from two different manufacturers. Somehow, he knew I was getting ready to ask him to interpret a particular set of coded numbers in one of the booklets. "That won't help you either," he said.

Many word choices began to form on the back of my tongue—none longer than four letters.

"Here's the deal," he said. "Do you have a long battery or a short battery?" I did not have the faintest idea, but the dead battery from my truck was in the trunk of my car in the parking lot. "Go measure it," he said. "If it's long, pick one from that stack." He motioned to one of the stacks of batteries. "If it's short, pick one from that stack. They're all about the same. It just depends on how much you want to pay."

"Make it easier on yourself," he said. "Go out to your car and bring your battery in and you won't get the wrong size. By the way, take your old battery up to the checkout counter and they'll give you a five-dollar rebate."

Because I was now late for my next appointment and had already invested so much time, I decided to take his suggestions.

The heat outside of the store was unbearable and the potential string of descriptive words returned to my mind. I shut them out, knowing that my quest for the sacred battery was just about over. I took a shopping cart from the shopping cart corral and placed my dead battery inside. It was too hot and too dirty to carry all the way back in my hands.

I was about to re-enter the store when I was approached by a sixteen-year-old "associate". His job was to ensure compliance with OSHA standards and any other directions that his supervisors gave him.

"Stop," he said. Seeing the anger on my face, and before the expletives being held captive in my head could be released, he went on to add: "I'm sorry sir, but taking an old battery into the store is a violation of public health regulations."

"You've got to be kidding," I said.

"No," he said with a confidence that made me want to punch him. "It's a health hazard."

I could sense my autonomic nervous system begin to dysfunction. Luckily, the image of a potential newspaper headline passed through my brain: "Executive Director Assaults Teenager with Battery." That was enough—at least for the moment—to deter me from many possible cathartic behaviors.

"What," I asked, "do you think I should do with this battery?" I added that I had been advised by another store employee to bring the battery into the store so I could measure it and receive a five-dollar rebate—a rebate that was getting less and less important to me.

"Why would you do that?" he asked. "Just go over to the computer display and enter your truck model, and you'll get the number of the battery you need to buy."

Instantly, I knew he had pegged me as a fifty-year-old computer phobic. "I already tried that," I said.

"You must have done something wrong," he said. "That computer has an *Ineptium* chip. It's very reliable."

Some other newspaper headlines went through my head. I wondered briefly what would happen if I smashed the battery on the parking lot. Would they have to close the store? Quarantine the parking lot until the National Guard came and removed the toxic waste?

"Are you alright, sir?" he asked. His words brought me back to my dilemma.

"What do you think I should do?" I asked with the most civil voice I could muster.

He said, "Just take it to the rear of the store. There's a separate service department entrance. Take it in there and they'll give you a rebate slip." I regripped my shopping cart and began my journey to the back of the store. I couldn't help but notice all the signs in the store proclaiming, "Our customers are our *partners*." Thoughts of revenge were beginning to preoccupy me. I wondered, where does the manager live? How hard is it to sever the brake-fluid line on a car?

Finally, I made it to the service department. No one was behind the customer service counter. The teenager in charge of customer service was on the phone. I waited a few moments and took my shopping cart and battery over to the kid. "Hi, 'partner'," I said. Apparently, he felt the heat from my body even in the air-conditioned store, because he moved away from me. "I need a rebate slip," I said.

He said goodbye to his girlfriend and wrote me out the slip. "Are you buying a new battery?" he asked. I ignored the question and asked, "Do you have a tape measure?" "No," he said. I didn't have the energy to continue the conversation.

I walked over to the display of "How Are We Doing?" brochures, picked one up, laid it across my battery, and folded it so I would have the correct length.

I journeyed back past the teenage OSHA agent, resisting any hand signals, and went back to the batteries. Finding one that matched the correct length, I carried it to the checkout lane and was soon greeted by another cheerful teenage clerk.

I handed her the rebate slip and placed the battery on the counter. "I'm sorry sir," she said, "but you'll have to get your rebate slip validated at the customer service desk before I can give you the five dollars."

"Please tell me you're joking," I said.

"Sorry, you need to take it over there," and pointed to two customer service representatives.

I left the checkout aisle, walked over to the ladies and said, "I can't believe this, but the check-out person said I have to have this slip validated before I can get my rebate of five dollars."

"That's not right," she said. "We don't do that here. Why would we give you a rebate before you've purchased something?" I was about to say or do something I would later regret when she asked, "Who told you to come over here?"

"She did," I replied, pointing back across the store at the

young girl. "One of your employees."

Sensing the anger in my voice, she said, "I'll walk back with you—but don't be hard on her. She's new and hasn't been trained yet." We walked back to the register in silence and she told the teenager needing training that I was upset and could she give me my five dollars and allow me to pay for the battery.

I walked out of the store an hour behind schedule. But I had the right battery—I hoped.

With reckless abandon, I canceled the rest of my appointments and went home to put the battery in the truck. It fit perfectly. The engine started immediately after I turned the key in the ignition switch. I drove around for about an hour, cooling off and wondering once again why God was using me for target practice. Later, I began to think of all the training gaps and the disastrous circumstances of having an untrained staff.

By now, you probably have a greater appreciation of my interest in training.

 భ

The remainder of this chapter describes those practices, programs, and philosophies which make continual learning a reality at Trinity Services. This recipe for learning is not a prescription for every organization, however. Think of the following ideas as ingredients you can select and evaluate, choosing those bits that are helpful to you. Sort of a learningful *jambalaya*.

Formal Training Programs

The next three sub-sections consider the matter of management training, Pre-Service or induction training, and ongoing learning that occurs through In-Service training.

Any organization seeking to provide training to company employees must answer the first question of training: who should do it? In many organizations serving individuals with disabilities, the answer to this question is found in the existence of a staff development department that may have as few as one or two employees, or as many as ten or fifteen. The thought in this approach is that training should be done by staff members who "do training" on a full-time basis.

I believe this is a mistake and would suggest just the opposite. With few exceptions, the people who regularly perform the work for which the employee is being trained should do the training. So, I hold that staff development departments should be very small and primarily do coordination and resource support work.

At Trinity, forty or fifty staff members are involved in teaching both the required and optional staff development. This approach minimizes the chance that seasoned employees— those actually performing the tasks when the newly-trained employee arrives—will say, "That's not how we *really* do it here." As a result, credibility is strengthened throughout the organization. Another benefit is that the instructors learn a great deal in the process of training other employees.

Investing in such a process takes time and, in many ways, is more difficult than simply hiring a few people to teach classes. The results, however, are much improved and last longer. Learning as a corporate value is strengthened throughout the organization.

Circuit Training

Management staff is frequently overlooked when the subject of training appears on the corporate agenda. Primary concern is directed toward the direct contact staff—especially if there are numerous regulatory requirements and high turnover rates.

In many instances, managers are thought to possess all the necessary skills once they accept the position. Apparently, one does not need to practice being a manager—unlike teachers, for example, who must student teach before they take on a classroom independently.

Other disciplines also assume the need to practice and learn before doing. Included are such vocations as plumbers, carpenters, electricians, psychologists, and various therapists.

It would seem that anyone could be a manager. After all, what kind of training, practice, or experience do you need to tell someone else to do something?

Quite frankly, this thinking scares me.

Nearly two years ago, Trinity initiated Circuit Training in an effort to help develop staff members in management and leadership positions. Management staff was surveyed on the areas in which it felt further information or training would be helpful. With such topics in hand, Trinity's executive committee divided the staff evenly among themselves into small groups. Groups were heterogeneous and so managers were working with staff members from across the entire organization. Each executive committee member served as a facilitator for a small group, including myself. The groups rotated from one member to another during the course of twelve months.

Once again, corollary gains emerged. A greater feeling of one organization—rather than twelve separate organizations—was strengthened. Employees were able to practice problem-solving approaches in their jobs.

The first session tackled the issue of authority. Prior to each discussion group, written materials were shared and read; the groups met for three hours.

A similar seminar was conducted each month, structured as the first one, but pertaining to other timely topics such as, "Fairness in the Workplace" and "Leadership Styles." Thus, Circuit Training was born and has since become an integral part of Trinity's approach to management training and maintaining good relationships among employees and between employees and program participants.

This kind of inter-departmental education filled a need to build rapport between program directors, managers, and staff of Trinity. Ensuring that people are resources for one another requires that they not only know each other, but have an understanding of each other's program areas, their problems, and how they work.

Circuit Training benefits the agency at every level and across every department. Through the various activities which occur at these sessions, all participants are exposed to different perspectives, air out their problems, make new friends, hone leadership skills, and reaffirm their commitment to the people Trinity serves.

A recurring theme throughout the sessions deals with different methods of leadership in an organization and the variety of results these methods can achieve. One of Trinity's program directors relates an anecdote from a session, "We chose leaders to lead their groups in various styles. The groups' project was to make snowflakes, and the results were incredible. One group made a ton of little snowflakes all the same, another just a few, but beautiful ones, another ugly ones—all depending on how the group was led."

The long-range goal is to help managers learn leadership concepts which are helpful in leading their respective teams.

Since its beginning, Circuit Training has evolved to fit Trinity's needs. The sessions now are held every two months, and the executive committee members have teamed up in pairs to present the new topics. No doubt Circuit Training will continue to grow as new needs arise. The outcome of this program is that managers and employees experience using each other as resources and expect to be continually learning.

Pre-Service
Every Trinity employee is scheduled into the first Pre-Service

session available after his or her date of hire. Direct contact employees attend the full forty hours of the program; other staff members participate in sections relevant to their areas of work. During this week of orientation and learning, all are introduced to Trinity's philosophy and organizational structure. Many of Trinity's executive committee members present various topics ranging from human rights to choice-producing environments to Trinity's budget. Often, this is the first opportunity some employees have to meet other leadership staff not directly involved with their respective programs.

To cultivate familiarity within the agency, Pre-Service instructors give tours of different program sites in the surrounding communities, accompanied by the *Sherlock* scavenger hunt. Now a Trinity institution, *Sherlock* was developed in an attempt to introduce new employees to the wide and varied components comprising the organization in an entertaining and interactive way.

Various facts, which reflect the core values of Trinity, as well as some trivia, are compiled in a booklet which must be completed by the end of the Pre-Service week. During the process of collecting this information, new staff members are introduced to a wide variety of employees, locations, and landmarks throughout the agency. During Pre-Service, group members are given time to collect the various information necessary to complete the exercise. As a result, newly-hired employees visit different residential sites for clues, meet with various program directors to obtain necessary signatures, seek answers from managers outside their own programs, and bond with each other as they inevitably collaborate to share answers and complete the puzzle.

Events throughout the week are varied and interesting. All the direct contact staff members are trained and certified in CPR during this time, as well as other pertinent and useful information staff members can incorporate into their work. Lectures are balanced with hands-on exercises. Much of the forty hours is spent within team-building exercises, emphasizing that the program participants are the beneficiaries of this teamwork.

In-Service

After a year of employment, direct contact staff members are scheduled to participate in a week-long learning experience. This is an experience employees look forward to, and they frequently inquire when they will be able to participate.

Again, the approach is to include staff persons from all program areas and to involve them in small-group learning activities. In-depth, updated information regarding Trinity is shared and written materials are distributed. Generally, a book, such as Dave Hingsburger's *i to I* (a sensitively written book about self-concept and people with developmental disabilities), is read and discussed. A conscious effort to stress values and purposes is made throughout the week.

In the middle of the week the groups gather around tables and discuss suggestions for making Trinity a better organization. After a year on the job, they have become informed and knowledgeable about the work they do, and feel comfortable suggesting new ideas and alternatives to the way things are done. The brainstorming generated here is a prelude to the final, most intense portion of the In-Service week.

The class breaks up into small groups. The instructions are simple: design a program to be implemented or work to solve a problem facing the agency. Class members spend the remainder of the week in these groups devising, researching, constructing, and presenting the final project. They are provided with whatever materials they need to complete it. On the last day the groups present their project to the members of the executive committee. The projects are ranked on a scale of one to five in areas of creativity, teamwork, quality of information, and presentation. An overall winner is chosen from the groups and the members are awarded gift certificates to area stores.

The high quality of these projects is consistent from class to class. The "Listening Ear" program discussed in Chapter Fourteen was initiated by a group of employees in In-Service. Other projects designed during In-Service classes include a video newsletter for the people served and their families and a benefit called "Family Ours" which provides eight additional one-hour increments of paid time per year, which employees can use to spend on family matters.

At Trinity, every effort is made to relate the skills learned and information acquired to multiple environments.

When teaching the fundamentals of behavior modification, for example, the instructor might point out that certain behaviors often get worse or more intense before they get better. This concept may be hard to grasp and a bit abstract for some participants, but when the instructor gives the example of a parent wanting their child to sleep through the night, it becomes more evident: the young baby, accustomed to being picked up and held every time he or she cries during the night, is likely to increase the intensity and frequency of the crying when this no longer happens. The crying will likely increase before the baby sleeps through the night.

Employee learning of this sort generates positive reactions and staff members often feel more competent and self-assured.

Communication Classes

In 1993, Trinity initiated communication classes under the direction of Bob Sandidge and Anne Ward, two experienced communication consultants and trainers. Everyone at Trinity, from the individuals served to direct contact employees and members of the executive committee has participated in these classes. The goal is for all of Trinity's staff to complete at least one multiple-week course.

Their approach is variable and intensive and calls forth much introspection and self-examination. Such issues as mindsets, positive reframing, and identifying personal outcomes are just a few of the subject areas explored. They emphasize the significance of learning and practicing from week to week. Participants are challenged to break free from habitual ways of seeing, hearing, and feeling and to view the world as openly and effectively as they can.

Sandidge and Ward represent the poetic influence at Trinity. The benefits of their consultations have been improved employee-to-employee as well as employee-to-program participant interactions and understanding.

It's easy to see how the smooth flow of communication facilitates the work of any service organization. These classes teach employees new communications skills while holding existing communication practices up to closer scrutiny. Making employees experts in interpersonal communications means improved interactions with persons with developmental disabilities. More important, it enhances an employee's ability to teach communications skills to individuals who rely on their ability to communicate for empowerment. Nowhere are employee development and individual outcomes more entwined than in the acquisition of communication skills.

Trinity Learning Center & Library

Every staff member of Trinity Services is required to complete eighty hours of training during the calendar year. This is a challenge to every employee, particularly those employees whose schedules make it difficult for them to attend full-day seminars. Trinity provides a variety of educational opportunities for staff development. The Trinity Learning Center and Library make it possible to provide the space, time, facilities, and materials for educating employees in a variety of opportunities year-round. The Learning Center, a renovated church with a large conference room and several smaller meeting rooms, makes it possible for Trinity to hold seminars of its own creation, or to bring in speakers such as David Hingsburger, Peter Kline, and Jerry Harvey, who are experts in fields such as disabilities, education, and management.

The Learning Center hosts Pre-Service, In-Service, *Understanding People* (a workshop developed by employees to educate staff on such issues as communicating with people who have substantial developmental or mental disabilities and dealing with and understanding challenging behaviors), communications classes, as well as any seminar, class, or conference with outside speakers and participants. Having a building devoted to training and education simplifies the logistical problems of seminars, conferences, classes, and meetings. And the physical presence of the Learning Center serves as a reminder to management that training and education are essential and continual. The Learning Center is consistently booked.

A complementary arm of the Learning Center is the Library. Providing books, audiotapes, and videotapes, the Library focuses on such areas as disabilities, leadership and management, psychology, self-improvement, and creativity. Employees may check out a wide variety of books and other materials which are required for their jobs. Books read or tapes listened to on relevant subjects satisfy a portion of each employee's eighty hours of annual training.

Trinity's Learning Center and Library combine to provide numerous learning opportunities for employees. The two are also a significant presence in the minds of staff, a reminder that Trinity places a high value on learning.

Learning Leaders

The term "learning leader" is borrowed from a discussion in Peter Kline and Bernard Saunders' book, *Ten Steps to a Learning Organization*, of trainers who head up and teach teams of employees in an organization.[1] The meaning of the term at Trinity, however, is very different. The position of learning leader arose from the need for direct contact staff members to learn the "whys" behind the services and supports they provide.

Some time ago, the thought struck me that Trinity, like most other organizations serving individuals with disabilities, was very much involved in the business of teaching. It was, perhaps, our most important function—helping people, who tended to learn more slowly, acquire greater levels of mastery, whether it be in academic areas or skills needed in living. If this is indeed the case, I then wondered how much time was spent on actual learning. My subsequent investigation did not bring thoughts of winning the Malcolm Baldridge award into my head.

Every person served by Trinity had the proper number of learning objectives—some had five, some had seven, some had more. Being generous in my calculations, if one objective, for which data is being taken—often referred to as "running a program" (a phrase I detest)—takes fifteen minutes, a person working on five objectives spends one and a quarter hours a day formally trying to learn something. So what happens to the rest of the day? In the day program? At home before and after work? (I should point out that this observation ignores the question of the meaningfulness, relevancy, and usefulness of the data collected and even the question of learning effectiveness itself.)

With this concern over our commitment to a learning environment in mind, I was shopping at the local grocery store when I noticed a Trinity employee shopping with two individuals from one of the residential programs. I knew that learning to shop independently was an objective for many individuals, based on the goals in their Service Plans. So it gratified me to see a Trinity employee in action, that is, until I began to observe what was actually happening. The staff person would push the cart and point to the items on the grocery list for the individual to take from the shelves. It looked more like a shopping cart race to me than "learning to shop." It seemed that the staff member was simply trying to get through this "program" as quickly and painlessly as possible.

My immediate, gut reaction was to discipline the staff member (I could at least scare the applesauce out of him). But are the direct contact employees really to blame? It seemed more likely to me that something, in the translation from Service Plan to service provision, was being lost. After examining the problem with the executive committee, we came to realize that the program staff had difficulty communicating the learning rationale, significance, and subtleties of the Plan to direct contact staff. They could tell them what to do, for how long, and how often—but they had difficulty helping the employees understand *why*. It wasn't the QMRP's fault or the program specialist's fault, and it wasn't the direct contact staff's fault; if it was anyone's fault, it was leadership's for not recognizing the need for deeper and more extended teaching. After all, what do organizations that serve people with disabilities mainly do? They teach. And yet, our commitment to teaching the direct contact employees was far from sufficient.

And so the position of learning leader was created—someone whose full-time job it was to assist direct contact staff in learning how to teach certain skills and abilities in the proper, educationally correct manner.

The starting point for each learning leader is the individual. Learning leaders follow the program participants across all environments, engage in dialogue, and offer assistance to any staff member helping to carry out a learning objective.

By beginning with the individual, staff members do not feel as threatened as they might. They are not the focus of inquiry— the person being served is. The learning leader participates in the small groups that the individuals typically spend a great deal of time in. They also work with roommates and housemates.

Bringing the learning leaders on board has certainly strengthened Trinity's commitment to learning. As a result, many other areas of our functioning are being examined. Members of Trinity's staff are now investigating incidental learning and informal training. How can these moments of opportunity be maximized? When to take data, how often, and by whom? The possibilities of self-reporting and self-data collection methods are being pursued. Using periodic "testing" of the skills being taught as an alternative to the present system of data collection is also under review.

Learning leaders represent an area of recent exploration at Trinity. Their impact has certainly been positive. Their full value and contributions, however, probably still lie ahead as the organization continues to learn from this recent innovation.

chapter seventeen

Risk-Taking

"To conquer without risk is to triumph without glory."
—*Pierre Corneille*
Le Cid

T HOSE OF YOU WHO have reached a certain level of physical maturity will no doubt remember the days when playing marbles was a popular warm weather activity. I'm talking about a particular variation of the game—the one where you dug a hole in the ground with the heel of your shoe (smooth gravel was best) and won the game by shooting all of your marbles into the hole on your turn.

My friends sorted themselves into two groups and generally stayed with their preferred teams throughout their elementary school days. They either played for "funs" or for "keeps." (Such ground rules had to be established before the first marble was tossed.) Some kids only played for funs, either because they were risk-aversive, had only a few marbles to start with, or claimed to be following the religious teaching of their church. Other kids, however, only played for keeps, perhaps because they had more generous allowances, knew someone who worked at a flower shop (and so had an unlimited supply of marbles), or were simply very talented in using their thumbs and forefingers. They were the risk-takers of the playground.

As leaders we must be willing to take risks and, even though we may be a bit scared, be willing to, in the imagery of author and leadership consultant, John Gardner, be the first bird off the telephone wire. Risk-taking is playing for keeps. Those who want only to "play for funs" invoke the common excuses for avoiding action: *We need more data. The staff will never buy it. We'll lose our funding. I don't even know where to start. Now is not the right time. My boss will kill me.*

Risk-taking renews both leader and follower. To be alive is to risk something to gain something without knowing the outcome. Of course, risk-taking that doesn't calculate the potential benefits and liabilities is just as unhealthy as never taking a risk. But the risk-taking culture of most organizations can probably be determined by the way that top leadership answer the question, "How safe do I need to be?" The need for security, the fear of loss or rejection is contagious and spreads outward, stifling the creative urges of staff members everywhere. Rare indeed is the underling who is willing to take on greater risk than his superiors. The manager sets the tone for risk-taking.

In research reported by Azi Fiegenbaum and Howard Thomas in 1988 in "Attitudes Toward Risk and the Risk-Return Paradox," they found that "most firms may be risk-seeking when they are suffering losses or are below targeted aspiration levels. Conversely, they will tend to be risk-aversive following achievement of aspirations and targets."[1] This behavior follows the "quit while you're ahead" school of thought. I would argue that even in organizations that aren't particularly successful, but which keep their heads above water, risk-aversion is prevalent. Only in extreme cases of hardship or catastrophe are they willing to change—when they have nothing left to lose.

Self-Confidence

The ability to take risks lies in self-confidence. Successful risk-takers are not "lucky." Luck, in a good risk-taking situation, should have little, if anything, to do with the outcome. In most instances, capable risk-taking is seen as risky or daring behavior by outside individuals, but it is never considered that way by the person taking the risk.

Successful risk-takers gamble on their or their organization's ability to come through. Risk is internally controlled, never dependent on external factors or luck. The variables that lead to success or failure are known and controlled by the individual or organization taking the risk.

In *Mind of a Manager, Soul of a Leader*, Craig Hickman recognizes the value of risk and argues that, "Managers conserve assets; leaders risk them."[2] Nevertheless, effective risk-takers always minimize the risk. Probabilities of success and failure are calculated and considered. Every propitious gambler you've ever heard of—infamous underworld figures or celebrated business tycoons—were hardly gamblers at all. They bet their money on sure things—a fixed horse race, insider stock information, or their own talents and abilities. Risk-taking that does not consider the odds of success, the probable investments, and potential pay-offs is like handing the keys of the organization over to someone else and saying, "Here, you drive." Do you really want to rely on outside forces and chance when you could bet on your own ability?

Practiced risk-takers take responsibility for their risk. Likewise, they do not gamble anything that they aren't willing to lose. A person who risks his good name and self-respect, or the dignity of others is not daring, just foolish.

There is no secret to successful risk-taking. A lack of self-confidence leads people to either avoid risk entirely or to willingly give up responsibility and take careless risks by relying on luck. You can't ever eliminate risk completely—and taking risks is necessary for growth. But to be risk-aversive is irrational. It is to ensure losing rather than to chance not winning.

e/o

The following ideas have been practiced at Trinity with a great deal of success in fostering personal responsibility and the willingness to take risks by direct contact and managerial staff members alike.

Idea Notes

It is important that top management be willing to take calculated risks—organizational progress is impossible without it. But management staff must also be willing to let other employees take risks. Some of the goofiest, most off-the-wall ideas often turn out to be the most successful. In an environment of fear and risk-avoidance, these ideas will never see the fluorescent light of the office workday. That is a shame. One solution to a fear of bringing forth new ideas is Idea Notes.

Idea Notes are essentially what they sound like—notepads with little pictures of light bulbs on them and lines for writing ideas. Other than suggesting an idea, there really are no rules. The "Idea Note Box" is not locked and no one monitors it to see who's been submitting ideas. This is because there is no Idea Note *Box*. Ideas submitted directly to a manager, program director, or me are not anonymous. Employees are encouraged to take credit for their insightfulness and creativity in solving problems and exploiting opportunities.

One Idea Note, that embodies the notion of risking something to gain something, proposed the idea of granting meal money to staff members before they left on a trip. The employee who suggested it risked angering those in the finance office, who sweat over audit trails and find safety in having three to five copies of everything. The idea was debated and then implemented. The result is that employees, who struggle with their own concern over cash flow, feel trusted and respected. That employees might use the money for something besides food is irrelevant. To use or not use the money for meals is a matter of personal responsibility, not of corporate monitoring.

The Silver Bullet

With apologies to Coors Brewing and the Werewolf, Silver Bullets are an avenue of communication between every staff member and any manager, program director, or executive director. They bypass the channels of hierarchy and provide direct responses to employees seeking to know the reasons behind certain policies, programs, or actions.

A number of employees in one of Trinity's In-Service seminars pointed out that there were certain times when employees needed to have a speedy answer or an explanation for a particular action or policy. The concern was that an immediate supervisor might not be knowledgeable regarding the systems or implications of such matters. In addition, if a direct contact worker is having difficulty with a particular management policy or organizational practice, he or she can send a Silver Bullet to me or a member of the executive committee and expect a response to the issue within twenty-four hours.

In a way, Silver Bullets officially sanction going over your boss's head. It is a recognition that an employee's immediate supervisor is not *the agency* and that direct contact employees should have access to the leadership of the organization. It also puts pressure on middle managers to communicate more effectively. But employees only receive three Silver Bullets per year, so the message in the Silver Bullet has to reflect an important issue that has not been (or can't be) adequately dealt with at the program level.

An example of the power of the Silver Bullet came from a

direct contact employee who questioned the high insurance costs for employees in the organization. Specifically, she wanted to know why, with such a large employee pool (one that had increased two-fold in her three years), hadn't insurance premiums decreased? Although many steps ensued after the receipt of her Silver Bullet, Trinity eventually secured insurance coverage with a competing agency, saving covered individuals $28 per month, and families $104 dollars.

Jerry Harvey, in *The Abilene Paradox*, describes the plight of Ozyx Corporation, an industrial firm in need of a Silver Bullet and on the road to Abilene in the form of a dubious research project: "When asked about the project...the president, the vice-president for research, and the research manager each describes it as an idea that looked great on paper but will ultimately fail because of the unavailability of the technology required to make it work... Continued support of the project will create cash flow problems that will jeopardize the very existence of the total organization."[3] Yet the research project goes on. Why? Because each member of the research project team is afraid of the other's reaction to his opinion of the project. The president doesn't want to kick up his vice-president's ulcer. The research manager doesn't want to get fired because the president and vice-president are so committed to the project. Without delving into the psychological dynamics of this situation, it is clear that some forthright means of communication are sorely needed in the Ozyx Corporation.

If the research manager had at his disposal a Silver Bullet, he could ask the president, "Why, in God's name, are we doing this project?" He could also point out his reservations without fear of retaliation. As you can see from Ozyx, organizations that don't encourage a questioning and open workforce endanger themselves in the process.

Essentially, Silver Bullets reduce the risk involved in questioning and pointing out organizational deficiencies. It is an effective way of encouraging employees to take responsible risks.

Seeking Proposals for Organizational Improvement

A learning organization is constantly realigning itself, examining the inevitable gap between vision and reality, making plans to do things better tomorrow. It is a seeking organization, not just a responding one. New ideas or new ways of doing things are explored and implemented before they are read about in professional journals or shared in "How to Do It Better" seminars.

Learningful organizations are creative organizations that anticipate the need to change in a rapidly evolving world. The creativity described in these thoughts essentially emerges from the people who are carrying out the work of the organization on a daily basis. Many organizational improvements occur as a result of simple agreements between interested parties. Other changes happen through formal or informal meetings. There are other patterns of ideas, however, that exceed the model of, "Let's just meet and make a decision on that." One proven, helpful device is to provide all employees with a simple, one-page format for presenting their ideas for organizational change. It is important that the outline not be unnecessarily bureaucratic or overly complicated; the intent is to have free flowing ideas. Having a standardized instrument is useful in as much as the proposal being generated will include all of the necessary elements.

Developing a Proposal – Five Steps

1) *Show that there is an important unmet need.*

   An employee must demonstrate with specific examples that a need exists and that fulfilling this need is critical.

2) *Specify the objectives, the specific outcome which will significantly affect that need.*

   How does the employee propose to fulfill the need he or

she has identified? What are the specific goals of the program and how will reaching those goals meet the need?

3) *Outline a plan for accomplishing the objectives.*

The employee details the scope of organizational involvement, estimates timelines, forecasts expected results, and plans for adapting to unexpected results.

4) *Establish the capability of carrying out the plan in an efficient and effective manner.*

The employee must realistically assess the capacity of the organization to carry out the plan. What skills, knowledge, or talents does the organization need to accomplish the task?

5) *Specify the costs anticipated in carrying out the plan.*

In my experience, proposals for organizational change or improvement tend to overstate the value of the proposed change while underestimating the costs in terms of money, time, and effort. That is why this section of the outline is so important. Employees need to become aware of the economic side of doing things differently. This isn't to say that proposals can't result in financial savings, but too often staff members see only the program advantages and not the attendant costs. Staff should similarly be familiar with the concept of sub-optimization—there are no perfect solutions. A positive intervention on the one hand may create a negative impact on the other.

Creating an organizational culture that builds an expectation of personal responsibility for making suggestions and which instills this expectation into every job description is the ideal for a change-seeking organization. This expectation of personal responsibility, along with the acceptance of risk that goes with it, should be conveyed in the initial interview and emphasized from that day forward.

chapter eighteen

Recognition

"It takes a wise man to recognize a wise man."

—Xenophanes

R ECOGNITION IS AN OFTEN used and often misunderstood concept. If you see one of your employees at the Seven-Eleven and say, "Hey, don't I know you? You work at Trinity, don't you?" while, technically speaking, that is a form of recognition, it's not exactly what I'm talking about. More prevalent forms of recognition in organizations are the standard "Employee of the Month" displays which look a lot like the "Wanted" posters they hang up at the post office. I tried a variation on this theme in my public administration days, but found that employees didn't respond enthusiastically to a "*Worst* Employee of the Month" award, either.

Unfortunately, most recognition programs aren't much better. Programs conceived and implemented without accounting for individual employee differences are doomed to fall short of management's expectations. Organizations attempting to recognize their employees in a meaningful way should have short, medium, and long-range alternatives. These strategies might be identified as "programs," but the applications are individualized. For recognition to be effective, it must emanate from the relationship an employee has with his or her supervisor and co-workers. Some people are motivated by very private, personal notes; others respond more productively when acknowledgment is public, perhaps in a team or department meeting. Because individuals are different, the recognition programs must vary to each person for the greatest effect.

It is also critical to consider what the organization wants to recognize—outstanding individual performance? Teamwork? "Going above and beyond the call of duty?" Donna Deeprose, in her brief monograph "How to Recognize and Reward Employees," describes three reasons for recognizing employees:

"By recognizing and rewarding employees, management:
- Establishes an equity arrangement, providing employees with a fair return for their efforts
- Motivates them to maintain and improve their performance
- Clarifies what behaviors and outcomes the company values."[1]

Other recognition programs may fail because many so-called "rewards," upon which the recognition programs are based, are extrinsic to a person's job. If an employee views work as a means to an end—a reward of money, benefits, or time off—he probably derives little satisfaction from the work itself. The best way to reward employees is to give them jobs in which they can take pride and from which they can derive satisfaction.

Job Enrichment

Ralph Waldo Emerson once said, "The reward of a thing well done is to have done it." When it comes to doing something you love, he's right. I might take his notion a step further, as it applies to recognition. The reward of a thing well done, *is the opportunity to do more.* If an employee shows that she can handle responsibility with ease, give her more. If a direct contact worker resolves difficult situations well, give him the responsibility of teaching his coworkers how.

The rationale for many of Trinity's recognition programs parallel the theory of job enrichment, a term originated by the psychologist and management professor, Frederick Herzberg. Job enrichment recognizes that most of the motivation to do a better job lies within the job itself—not merely with an external incentive or threat (what Herzberg refers to as a KITA, or "kick in the ass").[2] When management offers such carrots as time off, bonuses, coffee mugs, and parking spaces for working more quickly or productively, the employees are not motivated to do better—management is. Staff members are motivated to get time off. An employee who loves his job doesn't want time off.

Job enrichment is more difficult than posting "Employee of the Month" signs and handing out "Go Team" key chains. Enriching the job descriptions of direct contact employees requires creativity, attention to their needs, and, perhaps most important, trust. It means giving some management responsibilities over to staff.

Trinity Attendance Bonus

The Trinity Attendance Bonus program (TAB) began in 1994 to provide higher wages for direct contact employees who are employed in residential programs. TAB is essentially funded by reducing the amount of overtime hours and the extra costs they create. After 120 days of solid job performance, a staff member earns the right to participate in the program. The worker agrees to a set of responsibilities in return for a one dollar-per-hour bonus. This bonus represents a fifteen or sixteen percent increase in pay for most direct contact employees and is added to any other raises in salary. Direct contact workers then become responsible for their own schedules—getting to work on time, calling off only in emergencies (and then ensuring that the change in schedule doesn't create overtime), tracking and updat-

Dilbert® by Scott Adams   © 1995 United Features Syndicate, Inc. Reprinted by Permission

ing their own training hours (CPR, In-Service, fulfilling the eighty-hour personal training requirement), scheduling their time, establishing priorities, and otherwise performing their jobs with care and professionalism.

Staff members are, in effect, given a promotion. The bonus—although an *extrinsic* motivator—provides direct contact employees a more livable wage. Providing a sufficient salary is essential and must be addressed first, before considering motivators that enrich job satisfaction. Those motivators enter the scene with the increased level of responsibility. Staff members gain more control over their work and are trusted to be responsible. It is significant to distinguish this approach from simply assigning more work, or from a promotion that ignores the basic needs of employees. More responsibility, a more varied and interesting job description—intrinsic rewards—combined with extrinsic incentives such as money or a raise in status, represent the most effective recognition programs.

TAB demonstrates a high level of commitment to the direct contact staff by management. It recognizes that these staff members are not expendable, like extras in an action movie; they are valued and developed. The TAB program is helping to reduce overtime costs, the expense of high turnover rates, and is improving the morale and self-esteem of the direct contact workers who participate.

Exemplars

At Trinity an Exemplar is someone who serves as a model or example to other direct contact employees. Each year, managers and current Exemplars nominate those employees whom they believe meet the requirements of a role model.

To attain the status of Exemplar, an employee must be a full-time, non-management employee for at least two years, display a positive attitude on a regular basis, have the respect of peers, program participants, parents or guardians, and people in the community, go above and beyond the call of duty, exhibit excellent work habits and a willingness to help others, and treat others the way they would like to be treated.

Trinity Services is dedicated to ensuring that each staff member who exemplifies the values and principles of Trinity on a daily basis and who serves as a role model to all employees be recognized. It is hoped that all non-management team members will attain this status. To reinforce this goal, the Exemplar nomination process contains no set limit on the number of employees selected. Anyone who qualifies for Exemplar status will be recognized. It is not mandatory to represent each program area. Employees do not compete with each other to attain this status. Exemplars are chosen on merit, whether two or twenty are selected.

In addition to a raise in salary, a $200 bonus, an Exemplar ring (which the Exemplars designed themselves), and recognition in local area newspapers, Exemplars become part of the agency's leadership staff. They are included on various committees, participate in seminars and workshops with management, and attend the annual leadership retreat. As excellent direct contact workers, they can teach managers a great deal about Servant Leadership.

Although they may eventually move into management, it is not the intent of the Exemplar program to remove model employees from the jobs they do so well. If an employee is recognized as a great direct contact worker by being promoted out of his or her position, management sends the message that direct contact work is of little value. Exemplars then are also removed from the environment in which they can be role models. Exemplars are models of employee performance at the most critical level of the organization. They must be nurtured, encouraged, developed, and recognized.

Faculty Status

Many staff members excel as subject matter experts. They are knowledgeable in such areas as Normalization theory, creativity, first aid and safety techniques, adaptive equipment, and specific disabilities such as autism. Because it is the premise of Trinity Services to have as many staff members as possible engaged in the learning process, it is possible for employees to achieve the status of faculty member.

Trinity has established many areas of concern in which it is useful to have in-house experts. Staff members who want to share their insights apply through their supervisors for consideration by the organization's executive committee. Once selected, staff persons make a commitment to stay cognizant of the best practices in their fields of expertise, to circulate appropriate readings, and be available for individual consultation. They also serve as instructors within the staff development department. Faculty members receive an annual $500 stipend for assuming this responsibility and are recognized in various agency publications.

Celebrations

Celebrating accomplishments is the other foundation stone of employee recognition. Enriching jobs and celebrating achievements are key to instilling employees with pride and the desire to perform to their highest ability. At Trinity, accomplishments are celebrated in a variety of formal and informal ways.

The Holiday Party

At the end of each year, the Trinity Holiday Party is an opportunity for the entire staff to celebrate its hard work and accomplishments in a formal but fun setting. This celebration recognizes and presents gifts and awards to outstanding managers, QMRPS, administrative staff, new Exemplars, and employees who have been with Trinity for various lengths of service.

The Taste of Trinity Overall Chef (TOTOC, for short) is also honored (Taste of Trinity celebrates a culinary theme with dishes prepared by staff volunteers and enjoyed by all other employees and program participants). The holiday party is always well-attended. Employees dress up, gather in a beautiful ballroom, and enjoy a wonderful meal, music, and dancing. A frequently overheard comment by spouses of staff members at these parties is, "I wish my company did something like this." The recognition means a great deal to those honored, and the practice of officially recognizing, rewarding, and valuing employees is meaningful to all who attend.

Trinity Insights

An employee newsletter can extol the virtues of the company and encourage employees to work more diligently, or it can include information that employees actually care about and read. The latter approach is embodied by *Trinity Insights*. Trinity's employee newsletter is written *by* employees *for* employees. It comprises pertinent news—changes in insurance coverage and upcoming seminars for employees—as well as celebrations of births, weddings, promotions, or other significant events in employees' lives. Staff members from throughout the agency produce *Insights* every month to reflect the concerns of the organization as a whole.

Lillie Leapit

A recent innovation at Trinity, Lillie Leapit reflects the desire to celebrate staff accomplishments year-round. By nominating fellow employees with Frog Grams, staff members participate in showing their co-workers appreciation when they have achieved something worth recognizing. Lillie Leapit, a staff member dressed in a big frog suit, surprises the selected employee with balloons and a frog pin, while reading the Frog Gram that details the person's accomplishments. The silliness, the unexpectedness, and the group celebration of a Lillie Leapit visit make it fun and rewarding for all involved.

"I Appreciate..." Notes

These note pads say, "I Appreciate..." and leave room for the note writer to fill in who he or she appreciates and why. At the bottom of the note the person's name is printed as on stationery. These note pads are available to all staff. A manager may give a note of appreciation to an employee; co-workers give each other notes; and employees may sometimes even give their managers or other leadership staff "I Appreciate..." notes. Recently, I received a note thanking me for responding to a Silver Bullet.

That employees are recognized with these spontaneous, personal notes is significant. One-to-one recognition that comes at any time of the year is just as important as public recognition that happens at the end of the year. That employees have the power to recognize their supervisors and each other may be even more meaningful.

ớ

Recognition represents how an organization's workforce is valued. If managers and executives are the only ones who receive recognition, it sends the message that direct contact employees are considered little better than itinerant workers who come and go, but aren't really "members of the family." If attempts to reward employees fall short of improving employee morale and commitment, give thought to what workers really want from their jobs. A social service agency shouldn't be a place where people work as a means to an end. Just as outcomes are necessary for the individuals served, a job should have an outcome. Hopefully, that outcome is more than a twice-monthly paycheck.

chapter
nineteen

Partnership

*"When clearly stated and understood, purpose provides something
even more important than direction. It releases in people the power of
determination to reach that end."*

—*Perry Pascarella & Mark A. Frohman*

I NDIVIDUALS IN AN ORGANIZATION determine how they
relate to one another. These decisions primarily unfold
on a person-to-person, employee-to-employee basis.
Whether people are cooperative or competitive, warm or dis-
tant, helpful or aloof emanates from interpersonal interactions.
These dyadic relationships usually impact only the two involved
individuals, with occasional spillover to others.

The focus of the Partnership Agreement, however, is at the
team level—in this instance, that team known as the executive
committee of Trinity Services. Eleven program directors report
directly to me and represent all of the key programs and support areas of the organization. This group meets every week with
me for two or three hours and provides the daily leadership to
all of the organization's employees. The meeting's agenda is
broad and represents the particular issues or concerns that any
member wishes to discuss. Systemic concerns are emphasized.
Any issue that might present an organizational precedent is fully
debated. Issues such as employee discipline, compensation levels, transportation practices, job titles, program budgeting, and
standards of care are all considered.

Organizational Role Models

In addition to improving organizational performance and increasing the achievement of outcomes for the people Trinity serves, the Partnership Agreement serves a second purpose: to provide a visible team role model for all staff members. If the leadership of an organization can operate collaboratively and not engage in such counter-productive behaviors as gossiping, scapegoating, and fault-finding, staff members will be able to observe and imitate a model of interaction in the executive leadership team.

I'm not claiming that team members never act competitively or in conflict with each other. But, it is significant to point out that each of these executive team members makes a commitment to work for the greater good.

The mission statement of Trinity reads, "To be a leadership organization in providing the highest quality, socially responsible, and cost-effective services and supports to individuals with disabilities so that they might live full and abundant lives." The executive group accepts these words as the foundation for their working together. The Partnership Agreement continually evolves to meet changes in the organization. It is formally reviewed and signed by all members of the executive committee each year.

The Partnership Agreement

Following are brief descriptions of the important elements of the agreement:

Meeting Attendance

A Partnership Agreement will not be real in the lives of the participants unless they adhere to its conditions and responsibilities. Being physically and psychologically present at the meetings is essential. A partnership meeting without several partners is not a partnership—simply another poorly-attended meeting. To repeatedly miss meetings is to fail to give the process its needed priority, which in turn, hinders the group from resolving important issues. Few members want to put themselves in that position.

The executive committee meets twice monthly without me. In these meetings, they can hammer out differences, examine specific programmatic or administrative problems, or plan to take advantage of newly discovered opportunities. I don't know, because I require no minutes or summaries from them. The point is they meet knowing I trust them to be productive in their cooperative endeavor.

Setting the Agenda

Responsibility for setting the agenda rests with every partner. Agenda topics may originate from one or more group members, from the weekly executive committee meetings, from the executive director, or from other agency leadership staff.

Communication

Partnership meetings emphasize dialogue—not debate—as the appropriate mode of communication. This emphasis also prevails outside of the meeting room.

In *The Fifth Discipline*, Senge explores the meaning of the word *dialogue*: "There are two primary types of discourse, dialogue and discussion. Both are important to a team capable of generative learning, but their power lies in their synergy, which is not likely to be present when the distinctions between them are not appreciated." Senge defines discussion as a back-and-forth game of Ping-Pong, the object of which is to win by having your point accepted by the group—useful in critically examining different points of view. Dialogue's purpose, however, is to, "go beyond any one individual's understanding... In dialogue, individuals gain insights that simply could not be achieved individually." This process of dialogue, says Senge, requires the suspension of assumptions and the ability to see our assumptions as *representations* of the truth—and not truth itself.[1] Only in this cooperative setting can individuals further their understanding and work effectively as a group. Although it isn't easy, Trinity's partnership team works toward this ideal in every meeting.

A good example of this kind of cooperative communication took place during preparations for an Accreditation Council survey. Partners visited program areas which they were unfamiliar with to observe their daily routines and critical functions. Assumptions about other programs would be nonexistent or, at least, different from those who are responsible for the programs on a day-to-day basis. The dialogue that followed became an exploration of how to use the observations in improving certain practices or policies.

That no member can read minds is understood and so partners are expected to voice their concerns and opinions—not only for the employees they represent, but for the good of the organization. Disagreements must be conciliated. Members negotiate collective recommendations and decisions through consensus.

Members share important information during the meetings. They also seek reactions to and receive feedback on proposed plans of action.

Receiving and Giving Assistance

For some reason, people find it easier to give help than to ask for it. This is true of Trinity staff members as well.

Nevertheless, because partners agree to seek assistance from one another—as part of their written agreement—they are increasingly able to ask for help, guidance, and suggestions.

Problems members bring to the group include staffing assignments, management issues, and clinical dilemmas. Group members sense when one member is experiencing difficulty with a situation. Members expect to receive help when they need it, and to assist others who need help.

Active Listening

A good listener seeks to understand what another person is saying—with his words as well as his body language. (The importance of communications training emerges here.) Effective listening requires time, energy, and discipline—something the group identifies as a value worth emphasizing.

Encouraging Learningfulness

The Partnership Agreement encourages the sharing of journal and magazine articles, books, recent discoveries in the field of disabilities and management, or even something as specific as a computer software application. Resources, information on seminars and conferences are similarly shared.

A commitment to learningfulness encourages looking beyond the readily apparent in the world around us. For example, a recent newspaper article detailed plans to convert a local U.S. Army arsenal into industrial parks, a veterans' cemetery, and a prairie parkland reserve. While the meaning of this was not immediately obvious, the partners soon realized that this project would create many job opportunities for people receiving services at Trinity.

An inherent part of a learningful culture stems from the previous discussion of giving and receiving assistance. The executive committee recognizes its need to learn, gain knowledge, and grow in certain areas. To this end, the partners schedule in-house seminars or invite an expert in a specific field to share his or her knowledge with Trinity.

Praising & Celebrating

If Trinity has a theme song, it is "It's Amazing What Praising Can Do." (Actually, a recording of this song was made and played for the leadership staff at the annual agency retreat.) Praising is not synonymous with flattery. Rather, it means to recognize someone for his or her accomplishments. Most of us could certainly use more of this kind of encouragement. And so, partners celebrate each other's significant accomplishments, as well as the achievements of staff members.

Servant Leadership

In the Partnership Agreement, partners are bound to "uphold and demonstrate the principles of Servant Leadership." As detailed in Chapter Fifteen, Servant Leadership asks that leaders serve their subordinates. What do the direct contact workers need from us in order to better serve the organization's customers (persons with disabilities)? What do the managers need from us in order to better serve the direct contact workers? And so on. Including Servant Leadership as a primary tenet of the Partnership Agreement signifies the importance of this philosophy at Trinity.

Are We Getting in the Buick?

This reminds the group members to ask themselves and one another: "Are we doing what we *really* want to do. Or are we going along because we think it's what everyone wants?" As Harvey's *Abilene Paradox* reminds us, it is impossible to encourage honesty enough. Hopefully, this agreement, along with Trinity's overall culture, assists members in having the courage to tell the truth.

Conflict Resolution

The agreement ends with these words on resolving disputes:

"It is further acknowledged that, occasionally, conflicts occur. The executive partners agree to the following action: The partners involved in the disagreement will meet privately to discuss and resolve issues. In the event that this process does not produce a resolution, the matter will then be brought to the next partnership meeting for review and further discussion. If, at this point, the issue is still unsettled, the disagreeing partners will, together, seek counsel from the executive director regarding the issue."

The commitment to this process ensures that partners in conflict do not declare war on one another and "bad-mouth" each other to the employees in their departments. Instead, they seek to resolve the matter between themselves. The organization thus avoids interagency battles in which valuable resources are wasted in unproductive, and even destructive, activities.

In resolving disputes, I expect agency leadership to reach agreements based on trust. When entering into agreements, I am wary of the word "contract." Contract implies a lack of trust, the desire on both sides to secure an advantage and come out ahead of the opponent. An agreement, a covenant, or, as Charles Handy suggests, a "Chinese contract,"[2] allows both sides to gain in similar proportion and make the same amount of sacrifice.

Partners in Purpose

The Partnership Agreement enables the executive committee to focus its energy on collective achievement, as opposed to engaging in petty distractions. As a result, change takes place more rapidly and communication is open throughout the organization.

The executive committee and I have developed this agreement during the past four years. We are now trying to bring this type of agreement to other levels of the organization, to reinforce the principle that every member of the agency is in partnership to accomplish a common goal. Helping persons with disabilities achieve their outcomes—or facilitating organizational outcomes of any kind—is a process requiring the active participation and commitment of everyone.

The keystone of partnership is personal responsibility. Choosing and decision-making lie within the authority of every employee. Each employee decides, chooses, and carries out meaningful activities. They are free to use their brains and, with this freedom, realize that they are really working for themselves and not for their bosses or top management. Employees who experience job ownership can't help but perform their jobs with more satisfaction and pride. This is when employees cease being seen as disobedient children by management and start becoming partners in purpose.

♣

N o t e s

1   [1] Charles Handy, *The Age of Paradox* (Boston: Harvard Business School Press, 1994).

     [2] Peter Senge, *The Fifth Discipline* (New York: Currency/Doubleday, 1990).

     [3] James Cribbin, *Leadership* (New York: AMACOM, 1981) 8.

     [4] Ellen J. Langer, *Mindfulness* (Reading, Massachusetts: Addison-Wesley Publishing Company, Inc., 1989) 33-35.

     [5] Langer.

     [6] Senge 71-72.

2   [1] Bernardo Bertolucci (dir. & story), *The Little Buddha* (Miramax Films, 1994).

3   [1] Cribbin 237.

4   [1] Elliot Jaques, *Requisite Organization* (Arlington, Virginia: Cason Hall and Co. Publishers, 1989).

5   [1] Shad Helmstetter, *Choices* (New York: Pocket Books/Simon & Schuster, 1989) 109-110.

     [2] Helmstetter 119-120.

     [3] Robert K. Greenleaf, *Servant Leadership* (Mahwah, New Jersey: Paulist Press, 1977) 29-30.

6   [1] Peter Kline, *The Everyday Genius* (Arlington, Virginia: Great Ocean Publishers, 1988).

     [2] Senge 3.

     [3] Big Bill Broonzy, "I Can Do It All By Myself", *Big Bill Broonzy and Washboard Sam*, (Universal City, California: Chess Records/ MCA, 1961).

8   [1] Martin E.P. Seligman, *Learned Optimism* (New York: Pocket Books/Simon & Schuster, 1990) 20.

     [2] Richard F. Elmore, "Backward Mapping: Implementation Research and Policy Decisions" *Studying Implementation: Methodological and Administrative Issues*; Walter Williams et al (Chatham, New Jersey: Chatham House Publishers, 1992) 18-33.

     [3] Handy 50-55.

     [4] Rhonda K. Reger, Loren P. Gustafson, Samuel M. DeMarie, and John

V. Mullane, "Reframing the Organization: Why Implementing Total Quality is Easier Said than Done", *Academy of Management Review* July 1994, vol. 19, no. 3, 565-584.

[5] Reger et al.

[6] Jerry B. Harvey, *The Abilene Paradox* (New York: Lexington Books, 1988) 20.

[7] Harvey 14.

9   [1] Jessica Lipnack, and Jeffrey Stamps, *The Age of the Network* (Essex Junction, Vermont: Omneo/Oliver Wight Publications, 1994).

[2] David Brown, *Managing the Large Organization* (Mt. Airy, Maryland: Lomond Publications, 1982) 112-115.

10   [1] Linda J. Hayes, Gregory J. Hayes, Stephen C. Moore, and Patrick M. Ghezzi, *Ethical Issues in Developmental Disabilities* (Reno, Nevada: Context Press, 1994) .

11   [1] Linda J. Hayes, personal correspondence, May 1995.

[2] Hayes.

[3] James F. Gardner, and Nancy MacRae, *Outcome Based Performance Measures* (Landover, Maryland: The Accreditation Council on Services for People with Disabilities, 1993) 11.

[4] Richard Bandler and John Grinder, *NLP Comprehensive* (Boulder, Colorado) 6.

12   [1] Hayes.

15   [1] Jaques.

[2] Herman Hesse, *The Journey to the East* , trans. Hilda Rosner (New York: The Noonday Press, 1956).

[3] Greenleaf 29-30.

16   [1] Peter Kline and Bernard Saunders, *Ten Steps to a Learning Organization* (Arlington, Virginia: Great Ocean Publishers, 1993) 149-151.

17   [1] Azi Fiegenbaum and Howard Thomas, "Attitudes Toward Risk and the Risk-Return Paradox" *Academy of Management Journal* March 1988, vol. 31, no. 1: 85-106.

[2] Craig R. Hickman, *Mind of a Manager Soul of a Leader* (New York:

John Wiley & Sons, Inc., 1990) 240.

    [3] Harvey 17.

18   [1] Donna Deeprose, *How to Recognize & Reward Employees* (New York: AMACOM, 1994) 2.

    [2] Frederick Herzberg, "One more time: How do you motivate employees?" *Harvard Business Review* September-October 1987: 109-117.

19   [1] Senge 241.

    [2] Handy 87-90.

Selected

Readings

Brown, David. *Managing the Large Organization*. Mt. Airy, Maryland: Lomond Publications, 1982.

Cribbin, James. *Leadership*. New York: AMACOM, 1981.

Deeprose, Donna. *How to Recognize & Reward Employees*. New York: AMACOM, 1994.

Elmore, Richard F. "Backward Mapping: Implementation Research and Policy Decisions." *Studying Implementation: Methodological and Administrative Issues*. Walter Williams et al. Chatham, New Jersey: Chatham House Publishing, 1992. 18-33.

Fiegenbaum, Azi and Howard Thomas. "Attitudes Toward Risk and the Risk-Return Paradox". *Academy of Management Journal*. March 1988, vol. 31, no. 1. 85-106.

Gardner, James F., and Nancy MacRae. *Outcome Based Performance Measures*. Landover, Maryland: The Accreditation Council on Services for People with Disabilities, 1993.

Greenleaf, Robert K. *Servant Leadership*. Mahwah, New Jersey: Paulist Press, 1977.

Hale, Roger L. *Recognition Redefined*. Exeter, New Hampshire: Monochrome Press, 1993.

Handy, Charles. *The Age of Paradox*. Boston: Harvard Business School Press, 1994.

Harvey, Jerry B. *The Abilene Paradox*. New York: Lexington Books, 1988.

Hayes, Linda J., Gregory J. Hayes, Stephen C. Moore, and Patrick M. Ghezzi. *Ethical Issues in Developmental Disabilities*. Reno, Nevada: Context Press, 1994.

Helgesen, Sally. *The Web of Inclusion*. New York: Currency/Doubleday, 1995.

Helmstetter, Shad. *Choices*. New York: Pocket Books/Simon & Schuster, 1989.

Herzberg, Frederick. "One more time: How do you motivate employees?" *Harvard Business Review* September-October 1987: 109-117.

Hickman, Craig R. *Mind of a Manager Soul of a Leader*. New York: John Wiley & Sons, Inc. 1990.

Jaques, Elliot. *Requisite Organization*. Arlington, Virginia: Cason Hall and Co. Publishers, 1989.

Keeney, Ralph L. *Value-Focused Thinking*. Cambridge, Massachusetts: Harvard University Press, 1992.

Kline, Peter. *The Everyday Genius*. Arlington, Virginia: Great Ocean Publishers, 1988.

Kline, Peter and Bernard Saunders. *Ten Steps to a Learning Organization*. Arlington, Virginia: Great Ocean Publishers, 1993.

Langer, Ellen J. *Mindfulness*. Reading, Massachusetts: Addison-Wesley Publishing Company, Inc., 1989.

Lipnack, Jessica and Jeffrey Stamps. *The Age of the Network*. Essex Junction, Vermont: Omneo/Oliver Wight Publications, 1994.

Lovett, Herbert. *Cognitive Counseling and Persons with Special Needs*. New York: Praeger Publishers, 1985.

Pascarella, Perry and Mark A. Frohman. *The Purpose-Driven Organization: Unleashing the Power of Direction and Commitment*. San Francisco: Jossey-Bass Publishers, 1990.

Reger, Rhonda K., Loren P. Gustafson, Samuel M. DeMarie, and John V. Mullane. "Reframing the Organization: Why Implementing Total Quality is Easier Said than Done." *Academy of Management Review* July 1994. vol. 19, no. 3. 565-584.

Schein, Edgar H. *Organizational Culture and Leadership* (2nd Ed.). San Francisco: Jossey-Bass Publishers, 1992.

Seligman, Martin E.P. *Learned Optimism*. New York: Pocket Books/Simon & Schuster, 1990.

Seligman, Martin E.P. *What You Can Change and What You Can't*. New York: Alfred A. Knopf, 1994.

Senge, Peter. *The Fifth Discipline*. New York: Currency/Doubleday, 1990.

Sims, David, Stephen Fineman, and Yiannis Gabriel. *Organizing and Organizations: An Introduction*. London: Sage Publications Ltd., 1993.

Snyder, C.R., Raymond L. Higgins, and Rita J. Stucky. *Excuses: Masquerades in Search of Grace*. New York: John Wiley & Sons, 1983.

Vaill, Peter B. *Managing as a Performing Art*. San Francisco: Jossey-Bass Publishers, 1989.

Index

ABOUT THE AUTHOR

Art Dykstra is President and CEO of Trinity Services, Inc., an innovative human services agency. Under his leadership, Trinity grew from about three dozen employees serving about the same number of people in 1987 to more than one thousand employees and thirteen hundred persons served in 2007.

The agency gained national recognition as one of "America's Best Nonprofits" and earned the Psychologically Healthy Workplace Award for Illinois for 2007 from the American Psychological Association.

Mr. Dykstra has published a number of books and articles. He has taught at the undergraduate and graduate level on administration, psychological testing and executive leadership. He consults and speaks to professional and governmental organizations on topics such as leadership, mindfulness, innovation and organizational culture.

Mr. Dykstra has served as president of the Board of the Accreditation Council on Services for People with Disabilities (now known as The Council on Quality and Leadership), the Illinois Chapter of the American Association on Mental Retardation (now known as AAIDD of Illinois), the Illinois Conference of Executive Directors, and the Illinois Association of Rehabilitation Facilities. He is the founder and chairperson of the steering committee for the National Association of QMRPs.

Mr. Dykstra attended Bethel College, then earned a master's degree in clinical psychology from Bradley University. He began his career as an intern at the Elgin (Illinois) State Hospital, working with persons with severe mental illness. Before joining Trinity Services, he served in several capacities, over the course of twenty years, at the Illinois Department of Mental Health and Developmental Disabilities.